Pride without Prejudice

An inspiring life

BEVERLEY PINDER OAM

Pride without Prejudice

An inspiring life

BEVERLEY PINDER OAM

Edited by Adrian Jackson OAM

Published by:
Wilkinson Publishing Pty Ltd
ACN 006 042 173
PO Box 24135
Melbourne, Vic 3001
Ph: 03 9654 5446

enquiries@wilkinsonpublishing.com.au
www.wilkinsonpublishing.com.au

Title: Pride without Prejudice

Hardcover ISBN: 9781922810755

Softcover ISBN: 9781922810762

A catalogue record of this book is available from the National Library of Australia.

Cover photography: George Haig, GPH Photography, in collaboration with Jay Town.
Back Cover photography: Anthony Leong, Modform.

Design by Spike Creative Pty Ltd
Ph: (03) 9427 9500
spikecreative.com.au
Printed and bound in Australia by Ligare Book Printers.

Contents

FOREWORD

By Father Bob Maguire AM, RFD

Some people have personality, some have character. Beverley Pinder has both.

Her personality is colourful, which draws people to her. She knows how to talk to anyone, to engage with them, whether they might be part of high society or living on the streets.

Her character? She is as tough as old boots. She grew up in a challenging environment, and whatever success she has enjoyed in life, she worked hard to achieve it.

What I like about the 'Councillor', as I still call her, is that she isn't one to just sit back and enjoy her success. She never forgets where she came from. She is always ready and willing to extend a helping hand to those who need it.

She believes in what I like to call 'communitarianism'. That is the philosophy that we would all be better off if we could become more involved in our local community, if the help and love that thy neighbour needs could be provided by the local community, for the mutual benefit of all in the community.

This book explains who Beverley Pinder is, and how she developed her views on the world around us. You could do a lot worse than read it, and give her ideas your consideration.

– September 2022

PROLOGUE

This book, like most achievements in my life, is a dream brought to life. A dream that re-lives many moments of intense torment, bitter setbacks, sweet joys and great successes – hopefully, with still more vivid chapters to be lived.

I have captured my early days in Ceylon in the '60s and reflected on my subsequent years growing up in Australia. This was a period that saw me evolve from a guarded and somewhat timid young girl into a young woman seeking to understand the vagaries of a nation that discriminated harshly against people with coloured skin and slanty eyes under the White Australia Policy of the 1950s and '60s. Putting this into words has presented me with a very complex albeit colourful picture. This is because eventually, I enjoyed a level of success in my career that would have been beyond my reach had I remained in Ceylon.

I progressed onto the world stage in the Miss Universe competition at the age of 23. It opened my eyes, and also my mind to who I could be, and how I could influence and help steer others. Later, becoming a public relations consultant and then a successful businesswoman, I flourished through accepting and understanding the 'power of me'.

Finally, taking all that I had learned and a newly-moulded, mature personality into the realm of local government and politics, I had the wonderful opportunity to continue using my strengths in connecting people and 'getting things done'. It is often said that politics is the art of compromise. Inevitably my time in local government involved some degree of compromise with my intrinsic values of 'communitarianism', something which is core to me. However, I am proud to say that I emerged from my political experience without having put my name to any compromise that I simply couldn't live with.

We all change and evolve with time and experience, with our environment and our contribution. My best, most rewarding times have been when I am giving back – to the community, my family and my mentees.

I have navigated a series of transitions in life, from poverty to charity, beauty queen to PR maven, politician to now when I am 'retired' from business and politics. Somehow, I find myself busier than ever, whether enjoying family time, immersing myself in community work, helping with organising and fund-raising for charities, or assisting others in business as an inspirational motivator, ideas generator and mentor. I thank God that I am now in a place that brings me much comfort and satisfaction.

Life is a good dose of what you are looking for. Never stop short of trying to attain that which you know is achievable. And then keep going – exploring your next steps and getting onto the road that allows you to realise your fullest potential.

I hope you find something here to inspire and power your lives.

Beverley Pinder

beverley@beverleypinder.com
www.beverleypinder.com

Chapter 1

CEYLONESE CHILDHOOD

I may have been a child living in Ceylon, but it didn't really feel like I was living there. Because from my earliest years, I had always known I was coming to Australia.

In Ceylon (which has been Sri Lanka since 1972), my mother drummed into me and my elder brothers, Errol and Sandy, that one day we would be living in Australia. The nation was so much on my mind as a child that I often tell people today that I was an Australian long before I set foot in the country!

There were huge advertisements in the newspapers, reading, *"Australia: The Land of Milk and Honey"* and *"Australia Wants You!"* Whether those ads were entirely true is open to question: to get to Australia, you had to pass the tests of the White Australia Policy. Australia wanted you, yes, but only if Australia was confident you would assimilate.

The knowledge that I would one day be living in Australia changed my whole childhood. Everything I did and said was based on what I saw as my future life in a land Down Under, which offered so many possibilities and opportunities for me.

Instead of continuing with my Sinhalese classes, which were compulsory for all students, I managed to get permission to do elocution classes instead. I wanted to learn 'how to be' in a way that would suit my new country. In this, I took my cues from Tazma, a wealthy auntie who I used to love being around. Unlike my mother, she held dinner parties and had a busy social scene happening at her house. I wanted to be elegant like her.

That's because my home life wasn't everything I'd have liked it to be.

After moving to Australia, I would be crowned Miss Universe Australia, head my own highly successful public relations firm for more than 30 years and be a hard-working and passionate City of Melbourne Councillor.

Not bad for a poor immigrant girl from Ceylon who grew up in a family of seven, sharing a two-bedroom rental house that was no more than an annexe in a large building. I was the only girl among five children; I arrived after Errol and Sandy, and was followed by Durand and Dillon. My parents saw nothing special about me. In our culture in those days, sons were more important, more valued, than daughters.

However, the male doctor who delivered me *did* see something special when I was born Beverley de Zylva on 14 July, 1955.

"You have a beautiful baby girl," he told my mother. "She will become a princess when she grows up."

His words became my dream: I visualised a crown made out of crystals and diamantes that I'd wear, the shiny crown of a princess. That was probably the last thing my Catholic parents, Olga and Irving de Zylva, thought was possible for me. The fact my dream came true in a new and strange country shows how things do actually work out, despite so many obstacles which could have held me back.

***

My mother and father were Dutch Burghers, a minority race in Ceylon, where nearly 75 per cent of the population was Sinhalese. The Dutch ruled Ceylon from 1656 to 1796, but the Portuguese, who had previously colonised the island, withstood the invaders' siege for nearly 60 years. Despite this, the Dutch propagated colonies of Dutch citizens dubbed 'Burghers'.

In the first 30 years of Dutch rule, the Burgher population never exceeded 500 people. Mainly employed as civil servants in the Dutch East India Company, they were given liberal grants of land, with the right of free trade, and were the only people allowed to own and run shops. In 1907, the Dutch Burgher community founded the Dutch Burgher Union of Ceylon, which still exists today. When I was eight years old, there were approximately 46,000 Dutch Burghers, making up less than half a percent of the population.

Incidentally, around 10,000 Burghers emigrated to Australia from the 1950s to 1972. Burghers continue to make a huge impact in Sri Lanka even to this day, always punching above their weight. Chief Justice of Ceylon, Sir Richard Ottley, legally defined the Burghers in 1883. They have European surnames and you find them in all walks of life. Although many were forced to study in Sinhalese once the short-sighted government abolished the English streams in schools in the '70s, Burghers continued to speak English at home. The 2012 Census recorded some 37,000 Burghers living in Sri Lanka – less than one fifth of 1% of the population. Nonetheless, they remain prominent in the top ranks of many professions, including politics, entertainment (most Burgher families will have at least one musical instrument at home), sports, education, literature, the arts and journalism. They tend to get along well with all nationalities.

Despite our Burgher status, our family didn't enjoy much wealth or privilege. In 1961, when I was six, we were living in a small house when we were evicted from a rental lease that had just started. Someone had done a deal with my mother and an auntie so that our family could get the lease, but the lease didn't last long. The owner decided we couldn't be relied on to pay the rent, because my father was a drunk (which, unfortunately, he was). He sent four big, tough Sinhalese men to evict us and they tried to attack my father. I hid in the wardrobe for what must have been half an hour, maybe longer.

We all ended up on the footpath. And that's where I thought we were going to live.

Ceylon had a temperate climate so that was what a lot of beggars did, many of them amputees. But instead, we found ourselves couch-surfing for several months. We got to stay at my mother's uncle's place. They had a rather big home, but they had several kids. Our family got one large room, in which there were a bed and some couches.

Mum's uncle was really good to us, as was her brother who came to visit us and help us out. I've always made a point, as an auntie, to be generous and kind to my nieces and nephews, and I learned that from mum's relatives. I also learnt then the importance of food – because it was so scarce! When I later went to school, I was known to share my food at lunchtimes, both because I wanted kids to taste my mum's cooking and because I had learnt to share so well during this period of my life.

Mum was keen to find a proper home for our family, and luckily, she did, before the months of couch-surfing became years. She was always the explorer, finding out what our next steps ought to be – and this led her to a two-bedroom annexe on a larger dwelling in Pamankada, a district overcrowded with sub-standard housing. Our house was one of the few made of brick, and even had a tiled roof, but it was still dilapidated in sections and had seen better days. However, my mother was a scrupulously tidy person, and always made sure it was clean and liveable.

The whole experience helped develop an empathetic streak in me for people experiencing homelessness, and it led me to also have a deep understanding of how circumstances can change so dramatically for kids and families.

***

We experienced some economic hard times, but my mother made sure the family was well cared for and there was always a meal on the table. Boiled rice was our staple, occasionally with lentils, which the locals called *dhal*, made as a curry and accompanied by finely-chopped green leaf salad or *malung*. I can still smell it! Sometimes, however, times were even tougher, and there was no money to buy extras such as meat, fish or vegetables. That's when we ate plain fluffy rice with a touch of salt water to taste and grated coconut. Still, no one complained; we were grateful not to go hungry, as others did.

My father was a senior train driver for the Ceylon Government Railway. Train drivers were well respected in Ceylon, and many of them were Burghers who lived in designated railway housing areas like Mount Mary. My father was seldom home because of his extended shifts driving long distances on the upcountry line to Nanu Oya and Nuwara Eliya, and along the south coast to Matara. When he came home after being away for many days, he was irritable and sought solace in alcohol, usually an intoxicating spirit called *arrack*, which most Sri Lankan train drivers drank in those days. Distilled from coconut, arrack could be up to 50 per cent alcohol. And, while it wasn't cheap, it was much cheaper than the whisky, brandy, gin and rum imported for the upper classes.

While in his inebriated stupor, he often became violent to us. When he returned from days of work, he would inevitably be drunk – and have very little or no money. Not just because he'd spent it on alcohol, but also because he'd given it away to people who he thought needed it more than him, or he'd been so drunk he was pick-pocketed. Arguments would ensue with mum and, after they'd been together in bed, too often it ended up with him beating her. So, despite my father having a good job, we lived below the poverty line.

I knew he was hitting mum, but the boys were always playing outside and I think only my second eldest brother, Sandy, knew mum was being bashed. As a child, I didn't understand why it was happening. Obviously, there were fights over money. Later, after my father died of a brain tumour when he was 53, I realised that would have been growing in him for a long time, probably affecting his moods and behaviour.

I know that when he was on his deathbed and mum was looking after him, he would suddenly throw plates of food without warning. But, when he and mum were younger, there were also fights because my mother had a jealous streak. My father was a very handsome man and, despite being a violent drunk, he was a charmer. That's a heady mix – and a recipe for a volatile relationship, to say the least.

Sri Lankans love to dance in big halls with big bands. If a woman who had her eyes on dad came up to him and said, "Come on, Irving, let's have a dance", he would. When we got home that night, mum would be like a firebrand. She was possessive and would go to great lengths to show that my father was hers. And then the violence would start at home after a dance.

The same battles followed us when we later moved to Australia. There was a gorgeous redhead called Edith next-door to us when we lived in St Kilda. My father would go down to the courtyard and have a beer with her to, in his words, connect with "the life and the people". He would come back and mum would be jealous and there would be blue murder. I could never see anything wrong with it, but mum used to get jealous. That was no excuse for his violence, but it didn't help the situation. I've worked hard in my life to avoid letting jealousy control my actions.

My father also beat his children, and I think my eldest brother, Errol, suffered the most. I probably copped the least of his violence. I kind of looked like dad a bit, so I think he associated me with his family more than he did my brothers, there was more of a familial bond. He would shake me and, once, he lifted me off the ground by my ponytail; he thought I was responsible for Sandy falling over and cutting himself.

"Why didn't you tell me?" he shouted, but I couldn't say "Because at that same time you were busy bashing mum!"

This violence continued throughout our family life. I remember wanting to run away from home when I was about 16, but I couldn't go through with it. Mum was always saying she was going to run away, but she never did. Still, it was destabilising for me to keep hearing her say it.

Especially when we were in Ceylon, a man beating a woman didn't have that much of an impact on me in a purely social sense. Women were relegated anyway, we lived in a male-dominated household, and I think I grew up thinking this was natural, the way things were. But I also knew that my aunt and uncle – my mother's older sister and brother – didn't have physical violence happening in their households. I spent time with my auntie, and it didn't happen there. Going on holidays to her place was like a gift from God; I couldn't wait, it was a different way of life.

I know family violence's ramifications on my life have been deep and hurt me very much. I can feel diminished in certain settings and it has made me feisty around volatile situations. I can be misconstrued as having tantrums, and I think family violence also creates in a person a deep sense of how unjust life can be. Clearly, my mental health suffered as a child and that has continued through the rest of my life.

I have seen a psychologist for a long time, but I stop when I feel on top of the world. Then suddenly something will come crashing down on me and I regress. But I have always believed in having that professional expertise to help me pause and have that chat to get stabilised. It's very hard to talk openly about it and even now to write about it. But I know it's vital to seek professional advice for mental health issues.

I don't subscribe to Buddhism, but I do subscribe to the principle of detachment. Not being too attached to anything, and not even anyone. So, in a way, I learnt to see everything as dispensable. I think that's why later in life I started my own business; I didn't want to be dispensable.

And that's probably where my controlling behaviours started as well; I needed to *know*, I needed surety.

I'm so glad that in my life, in my step-parenting, I have been able to be a positive influence. And I think seeing my aunties and uncles model a different way of life really helped me.

***

As well as physical abuse, my father would also pick on everyone's minor errors and omissions and give us a tongue lashing. I remember my brother Sandy copping it after my father found he'd shown more than a passing interest in our Sinhalese neighbour's daughter.

"We are *Burghers* and we must not mingle with other races in affairs of the heart!" he growled. "Besides, you are only 14 years old and shouldn't be thinking of girlfriends. When you are old enough, you should be seeing Burgher girls because you will be marrying one of your own kind. Not a Sinhalese, Tamil or a woman from any other race."

When Sandy started protesting, my father drowned him out with a guttural, "Shut up!" Sandy knew what would happen if he didn't, so he promptly obeyed.

All this violence came, however, from a man I found several times engrossed in Sandy's cowboy comics. He seemed just a simple child in those moments, and not someone who could be so violent to us all. And certainly not someone who, as he claimed one day, could kill someone.

***

My father came home one Saturday morning after working a shift to Kandy. He was preoccupied and distant when he walked in, throwing his Gladstone bag on the dining table. We children kept our distance, as usual, while our mother spoke to him, trying to calm him. He ignored my mother's entreaties, sank into the sofa and didn't speak for a few minutes. Then his words hit us like a thunderbolt.

"I killed a man yesterday," he muttered.

Our mother gasped and shooed us away to our bedrooms. *My father a murderer?* I thought as Sandy dragged me away. And, although we were in our bedrooms, we trained our ears to gather bits of our parents' conversation.

"But why, how, Irving?" my mother asked animatedly. "Why did you do such a thing?"

"He jumped in front of my bloody train just after I'd negotiated the difficult Kaduganawa climb."

Our mother sighed with relief. "So, it was an accident . . . you didn't physically *kill* the man?"

"No, I am not a murderer, but I still killed him. The damn fool thought he could make it across the tracks before my train reached him," he said, sounding somewhat relieved. "It was a long train. I simply didn't have enough time to stop it."

My father muttered that the man had been a *modaya*, which is Sinhalese for "fool". Then he went on to spill the gory details.

"He was decapitated – the head severed from the neck and one of his arms must have flung into the dense growth lining the track. I told Piyadasa, my fireman, to take the dead man's head down to the nearby village to try and have it identified. The fool picked up the bloodied head by the hair and walked straight to the small village, swinging it as if he was carrying a shopping bag! When the ignorant villagers saw him with the dead man's head, they screamed and fled as if they'd seen a ghost."

I shuddered as I heard all this; it was so vivid that it felt as if it were happening in my bedroom. I opened my door just a little and chanced a peek at my parents.

"I need a bloody drink," my father said, and he reached for his arrack. "That was my first accident in 25 years, and it happened to be an idiot who didn't seem to give a damn about his life," he said, gulping the drink and pouring another. My mother shrugged her shoulders in disgust at his drinking and went about her daily chores.

I can't help thinking how much that incident must have affected my father, what it did to his soul.

***

With an often absent, distant, intoxicated and abusive father – and brothers into cricket, rugby and cycling – I felt isolated, a girl not welcome in a boys' domain and their rough sports. So I decided to turn my isolation into taking on a protective role; I would watch over my brothers and make sure they didn't fall over. I developed a strong sense of responsibility for my family, a kind of maternal instinct.

My elder brothers, Errol and Sandy, were doing exceptionally well at St Peter's College. Errol was showing his athletic prowess, excelling in sprints and long jump, while Sandy carried the family's honour with his academic brilliance. We made many trips to St Peter's College to attend Sandy's award ceremonies, applauding him as he walked up onto the stage to claim prize after prize. It got so that I was able to sing his college anthem off by heart!

Mum made sure Errol had the best serves of food at mealtimes, so that he would be in peak condition for his athletic events. Occasionally, there was a total of two soft-boiled eggs for us children for breakfast, and Errol had one of them. Even then, I was only allowed the white while the boys shared the yolk.

While my brothers were favoured, as I grew they took a greater interest in me. Where once I had seen myself as their protector, they started to become protective of me. My safety became their top priority; I was never allowed to leave the house and go to the shops alone – one of my brothers would always accompany me. As a result, I seldom mixed with the Sinhalese people and actually didn't speak any Sinhalese. So, when I started school, I was in for a shock when I saw how some people reacted to me.

***

When I turned five, my parents sent me to the strict but popular St Lawrence's Girls' Catholic school in Wellawatte. The school, which used to be co-ed, became girls-only in the '60s. It was wedged between a collection of shops lining the main highway, Galle Road. Wellawatte had a high population of Tamil people, and Tamils and Muslims owned nearly all the shops.

My mother took great pride in dressing me in good clothes. My white school uniforms were neatly ironed and I enjoyed the attention that people paid me. I usually travelled to school with my brothers because St Peter's College was only a mile up the main road from my school. But one day my brothers left early for school and I had to take the bus alone.

Most Sinhalese, Tamils and Muslims had darker complexions and, while I was waiting for the bus to arrive, I noticed a man with a dark complexion staring at me. He was muttering under his breath in Sinhalese and the only word I understood was *suddhi*, a mildly derogatory term for women with the light skin tone I had. I ignored him, but for some reason he continued to swear at me. Then he walked past and suddenly spat something utterly vile at me. He must have been chewing a betel nut, a common sight in the country, because his spit splattered my clean white uniform into an ugly red. Moments later, his bus arrived and he boarded it. I was in tears because my beautiful uniform was ruined. To make it worse, this unknown man even gave me a mocking grin as he swung up onto the footboard of the crowded vehicle and made more rude signs at me.

I dashed home in fear, messed up and feeling terrible that, just because I had a different skin colour, I could be treated so horribly.

It was definitely better to walk to school with my brothers because, when I was a few years older, I had another bad experience riding the bus to school.

I always had a fear of Buddhist priests. It could have been a kind of religious bias because it was the '60s; religious tolerance wasn't a very well understood concept; and I went to a Catholic school. It could also have simply been because they were older men and, due to what was happening at home with my father, I was developing something of a fear of men.

The Buddhist priests in their saffron robes rode the bus with everyone else – and I mean *everyone* else! This was more than 60 years ago and the buses were completely chock-a-block. This day, I was standing and was thrown around a bit as the speeding bus swerved and a Buddhist priest, about 35 years old, caught hold of my waist and put me on his lap. At first, I felt safe because someone was hanging onto me, though I began to feel more uncomfortable and, when I got home that night, I told mum I was a bit scared on the bus because it was very jerky and swirly. I told her a Buddhist priest helped me, but it was very uncomfortable because he had his walking stick underneath me. The priests used to carry staffs, so I suppose that was why I presumed that what I'd felt was his staff. Mum just brushed me off, as mum always did, and that was the end of it. But I knew something wasn't right.

From that day, unfortunately, if I see a Buddhist priest coming, I walk the other way – and I can't look at the saffron colour. And I wonder about the experience from that priest's perspective. He would have known I was Catholic; I had my tie on and was dressed in white. Was it a special thrill for him, a Catholic girl on his lap? Or was it something he could do without fear because of the respect the robe gave him?

What this harrowing experience did was help me develop a very handy 'antenna' to keep me safe from those who could harm me, sexually or otherwise. I was always aware of men looking at me as a child and teenager, and I kept an emotional distance; I found a way to detour in my mind. I became very good at that. I had no other experiences like the one with the priest, so I think that antenna was a very good thing to develop when I did.

***

While my lighter skin tone sometimes meant I was attacked or hassled on the streets, it was fortunately very different at school. Mother Eleanor, the Principal, made me and my friend Romany Jansen her favourites – she was always calling upon us to do special tasks.

She also regarded us as two of the smartest kids in the school.

I excelled in maths, English and elocution, and I was also good at netball and dancing. I finished my classwork quickly, then asked around if anyone needed help. Sometimes, I would hold my work up for those behind me to copy because I wanted everyone in the class to do as well as I did!

If you surveyed 40 of us today from that class, everyone would say we didn't have much money. But I know our family's circumstances were very different due to the family violence we regularly endured, in a male-dominated household where poor mum was constantly striving to put food on the table.

Reflecting on my mother's life, I marvel at her endurance. When she was 13, mum was almost on her deathbed with rheumatic fever. Having survived that, she enlisted in the Navy at 15. She never had it easy before marrying Irving when she was 21. And from then on, she was forever working hard as a wife and mother. She was 31 when she gave birth to her fifth child.

Perhaps I was inspired by her example, I always worked hard at school. I was a terrific reader of Ceylon's mother tongue, Sinhalese, but I preferred to do elocution and, because I was one of Mother Eleanor's favourites, I didn't have to pay much attention to studying or speaking Sinhalese. During elocution class, I was called up to show others the finer points of enunciation and presentation. Many of my classmates marvelled at my memory and how good I was at remembering detail. It's a skill I feel I've retained to this day.

I helped several girls who had difficulty learning English. To my good friend Marina Fredricks, I said, "Don't worry, I will look after you." I had this inner resolve, a feeling I could withstand things for her and help her overcome whatever opposition she faced. Tenacity and resilience were building in me, making me seem fearless.

And I had to be – when puberty came along.

I recently helped Marina with the courage she needed when she cared for her husband (also a good friend) as the debilitating Lewy Bodies disease took him away from us and into God's arms.

Chapter 2

TEENAGE TRANSITIONS

I had just turned 11 and children in Ceylon at that time didn't receive sex education. I noticed I was bleeding and I didn't know what was happening to me; I thought I'd done something wrong. I didn't confide in anyone and waited until the third day of the bleeding to talk to my mother.

She was in the kitchen making dinner when I spoke to her. She ushered me into my room and forbade me to come out. She rushed down to speak to our Muslim landlord and his wife, who had five daughters, for their advice. They summoned a local fortune teller who instructed my mother that, after seven days confined in my room away from prying eyes, she should bathe me. So, off I went to my room, with a yellow flower in my hair to 'ward off the evil eye'. When the seven days were up and the auspicious day for my cleansing arrived, a tin bath was filled with water and I was bathed facing east to greet the rising sun.

I didn't know it then, but this was a typical Sri Lankan custom strictly observed by nearly all families when their daughters reached puberty or became 'big girls'. This description bemused my cynical brothers who couldn't understand why I was called a 'big girl' when I hadn't grown at all!

With puberty, of course, came physical changes and I noticed boys often eyed me, particularly during sporting activities, although I barely took any notice. I simply wasn't one of those lovesick teenagers who craved for stolen kisses.

But there was one Burgher boy, Stewart Wright, who I heard had a crush on me. In fact, he passed on a photograph of himself to my friend Sharron to give to me. I took it, mildly flattered at his interest, but didn't pursue it, except for an occasional smile when our paths crossed. He was a good athlete and I saw him training at St Peter's College's sports arena, but there were no secret rendezvous or kisses at matinees in the local cinema. I was enjoying an uncomplicated life with the goal, even then, of making it to the top one day. Romance and teenage crushes were not a priority because I was looking forward to living in Australia – and the idea of 'making it' there.

***

Ceylon was granted its independence from Britain in 1948, seven years before I was born, and during my childhood it became tough for minority races like Burghers. Winds of change caused major havoc on the political scene; Sinhalese politicians wanted Sinhalese to replace English as the country's national language. English was, however, the medium of instruction in schools, and was used in all government departments and businesses.

In 1961, when I was six, I finally asked my mother why she kept saying, "We are going to Australia". She told me of the banner headline she'd read in a local English language newspaper: *"Sinhalese Only in 24 hours*". The Sri Lanka Freedom Party, in power since 1956 and led by Oxford-educated Solomon West Ridgeway Dias Bandaranaike, had promised the people that Sinhalese would become the national language.

Prime Minister Bandaranaike was killed by an assassin's bullet in 1959 and his politically-inexperienced widow, Sirimavo Bandaranaike, took his place as the world's first female prime minister. Her government adopted a new constitution with "Sinhalese Only" as a policy. It became the country's official language and gave Buddhism a 'foremost place' as the faith of the majority Sinhalese people.

Minority races, such as Tamils, Muslims and Burghers, who felt ostracised because they were not Buddhist, also had to show proficiency in

Sinhalese or face dire consequences in their jobs. In the new ideological climate, my four brothers and I soon found it difficult to pursue our studies because of the extra focus put on Sinhalese as the medium of school instruction. Even my father was faced with the task of passing a proficiency test in Sinhalese at his workplace. So, on 27 April 1967, my parents decided to put in their application for immigration to Australia.

In the words of Robert Louis Stevenson, for me and my Dutch Burgher Catholic family it was a case of: "Home no more home to me/Whither must I wander/Hunger my driver, I go where I must."

But getting to Australia was by no means going to be easy. First, we would have to negotiate Australia's notorious White Australia Policy. The rigorous criteria meant you had to prove that more than 70 per cent of your bloodline was of European descent. All the Burghers, who filed their migration papers during this White Australia Policy time, had to trawl through the records of their churches to find records of their grandparents, great grandparents – and even great-great-grandparents – to trace the genealogy, which was then submitted to the Australian Embassy as a part of their migration papers. I recall mum visiting cemeteries in various churchyards to confirm the dates of birth or death of several forebears.

However, even if you did meet the bloodline requirements, some applications were rejected without explanation. Many did not know that there was a quota system that applied to countries like Ceylon. This was simply another hurdle that the Burghers had to get past in order to move out to 'greener pastures'.

***

Australia's restrictions to immigration began with anti-Chinese legislation during the 1850s goldrush, but the *Immigration Restriction Act 1901* enshrined the White Australia Policy in law. The legislation began to lose its sting in the 1940s when reforms encouraged non-British and non-white immigration. The White Australia Policy was gradually dismantled by the Government of Harold Holt in the late 1960s, and race-based immigration criteria were discarded by the Whitlam Government in 1973, and finally made illegal by the *Racial Discrimination Act 1975*.

But when our family was planning to emigrate to Australia, the White Australia Policy was still a big hurdle for us to overcome.

We had the advantage of the fact that our skin was comparatively light in tone. With that helping us, passing the test came down to how we dressed, the intonation of our speech – even the colours of the clothes we wore to the interview. All of that went into a points system, and the aim of the whole test was to prove whether we would be able to integrate when we arrived in Australia.

My father was also able to prove he was a British subject of European descent, and my mother was certified as a Ceylonese of European descent. This all helped our case and, six months after we applied, we received a letter from the Australian High Commission, informing us that we were eligible to enter Australia before 21 October, 1968.

At last, all my mother's words – and my dreaming – about going to Australia were set to come true.

My father, 39, at the time, filed his papers for retirement from the Ceylon Government Railway after 21 years of service. He received a minimal pension, so we had to borrow the money to pay for our airfares. A well-known banker, Brindley Jansz, keen to get his money out of Ceylon, offered us a loan, which was accepted gratefully.

My mother decided to pull me out of St Lawrence's a few months before our departure date so our family wouldn't have to pay another term's school fees. It was a sad and abrupt end to my wonderful years at the school, and I never really had a chance to say goodbye to my friends.

I was 13 when we left the land of my birth. It was becoming more and more confused, with ethnic rivalry resulting in bloodshed from racial riots caused by the government of the time. Many lives were lost in the frequent bloody clashes; and sadly, hatred took root in this predominantly Buddhist country. Murder and mayhem had begun to govern people's lives, contrary to the venerable Gautama Buddha's teachings of peace, harmony and *ahimsa* (respect for all living things and the avoidance of violence).

I was sad to leave Ceylon, especially my friends, but I knew that this was the start of a new and exciting life.

Chapter 3

A DOORWAY TO FREEDOM

We arrived in Australia at Essendon Airport on 2 October 1968 and, as we disembarked the BOAC aircraft, the first thing that caught my eye was space. Land stretched out endlessly. There was no traffic congestion, no ugly crowded buildings, and a sense of unhurried calm prevailed.

I was dressed in a sleeveless red A-line dress and black patent leather shoes. It was a chilly eight degrees in Melbourne, but the cold did not deter me. I saw the space that unfolded around me as a doorway to freedom, and I whispered to myself: "This is my home. I'm going to make it here."

It was a strange thing for a 13-year-old girl to tell herself, and I said it with an overwhelming sense of positivity. I had none of the apprehension that I could have been forgiven for feeling on this my first few hours in a new country.

***

Our first home was a three-level Victorian terrace in Dalgety Street, St Kilda, rented for the princely sum of $19 per week. It was fully furnished with fine Jacobean furniture; I couldn't have asked for a better start. For the first time, I had my own room, and I quickly put on the wall pictures of successful models and beauty queens. They were there to make sure I pushed myself to be the best and believed that success and a sense of belonging were within my reach.

It wasn't that I wanted to become a model myself, much less a beauty queen. But these were young women who were popular in Australia, I wanted to learn to dress like them, carry myself like them, so that I too could become popular in my new country. I craved acceptance.

My parents enrolled Sandy and me at Elwood High, and my younger brothers at Elwood Central. Elwood High was a wonderful experience because migrants were made to feel welcome. I made several good friends, among them Rachel Rovay, who would go on to become an esteemed visual artist. We have remained friends ever since, and she painted my portrait for the 2014 and 2016 Archibald Prize (see this book's second photo section).

I shed my puppy fat and began to turn into a young woman – and soon found I was attracting the young males at school. One of them, Oliver Blomberg, always made a beeline to be with me during the lunch break. I wasn't attracted to him, but I didn't want to embarrass him by spurning his advances. He must have misunderstood my coy smile and unusual accent because he was all starry-eyed until the next lunch break! Perhaps it was early evidence of the skills I later found I had in public relations, that ability to keep people happy and connected.

My father, however, was not particularly happy in Australia because he could not find a job on his beloved railways. His years of experience as a train driver in Ceylon earned him respect from his superiors and his colleagues. But in Australia, union policies meant that his experience and qualifications were not recognised. Instead of working on trains, he had to settle for a job in the boiler room at Larundel Hospital, followed by work with Carlton United Breweries and then, years later, an administrative job with H. C. Sleigh in Queen Street.

My father became very depressed about this change of career and status, and soon was drinking more heavily than ever. This led to more violent and abusive outbursts, which took a heavy toll on our family, especially my mother.

Meanwhile, I would go to bed visualising myself wearing a crown made out of little crystals and diamantes. That crown represented my vision to be referred to as an 'Australian'. It also represented my desire to achieve success in life. It was a pinnacle that would motivate me to face every new day with the determination that I could seize it, no matter what I was up against

At first in Australia, there were no major tests of my resilience; I was 14 and enjoying living in our house in St Kilda, so much more spacious than the one we'd left in Ceylon. I was doing well at Elwood High School; it was a fun place to be and I continued to make friends due to the school's openness to migrants. And, in my spare time, I stumbled into a pursuit that would take me around Australia and the world – and set me up for my future career.

One Saturday afternoon, I saw on television the then well-known Aboriginal activist and opera singer, Harold Blair. He was asking for young girls to enter the Junior Miss Victoria competition, which involved raising money for Aboriginal education and development programs, including providing kids with a summer holiday.

I loved summer holidays so the idea of helping out really appealed to me. It was the first time that my charitable streak showed itself and I got stuck into it: I worked hard to raise money by organising charity drives, fundraising dinners, car washing, barbecues and selling chocolates.

The competition was at Dallas Brooks Hall and, dressed beautifully by my mother, I fronted up on the day with a bag of cash – money that I had raised, probably about $900. I waited in line at the entrance to the Main Hall to have my name ticked off at a table presided over by Joy Snedden, wife of then leading Liberal Party politician, Billy Snedden. I had done my research; I knew who she was so that I could address her by name when we met.

I made it to the front of the line and Mrs Snedden asked my name.

"Beverley De Zylva, Mrs Snedden," I said cheerfully.

She searched and searched her list for my name. "I'm sorry dear, you're not on my list."

"Oh, Mrs Snedden, I definitely signed up for the competition, here's my money," I told her, proudly showing her my bag of cash. The penny dropped for her.

"Ah, you're in the Charity Section," she said, and I nodded. "Well," she added, looking me over. "You should be in the Beauty section, too."

So she scrawled my name onto the list for the 14 to 16-year-olds' Beauty Section.

And I won!

I'd always thought of myself as different-looking, too exotic to be beautiful. But I loved this turn of events. I thought, *Wow, this is all right!* I won a hi-fi system, which my brothers happily claimed as their own, and a modelling course at Helene Abicair School of Deportment.

All because I'd raised money to help Aboriginal kids!

From that day on, I kept entering competitions, but took my cue from Mrs Snedden and always entered the Beauty section along with the Charity section.

As exciting as all this was, however, I would soon have a major challenge to face, a period that I now think of as one of the worst times of my life.

***

By 1972, my parents had saved enough money for a deposit on a house and they bought one where they could afford: Springvale. It cost $14,500, and was a four-bedroom, brick veneer on a traditional quarter-acre block.

I was very upset to leave Elwood, having made so many great friends. My two younger brothers and I were enrolled at Springvale High School and this was where things changed dramatically for us.

Our move to Springvale coincided with Vietnamese and East Timorese people moving to Australia as refugees, and acceptance of migrants hadn't reached the level it had in Elwood. In Springvale, we were subjected to daily racist taunts.

Whereas in Ceylon I had been taunted because my skin was too light, now I was being singled out because my skin was considered too dark. Kids would say, "You're from Ceylon? Where the hell is that?" I was greeted almost every Monday morning with the comment from some boys, "So, how was the Corroboree on Saturday night, Beverley?" Even though I was 16 then, my parents were strict, and I wasn't allowed to go out on Friday or Saturday nights.

My brother Durand was nicknamed "tea bag" because of his complexion, while my youngest brother Dillon, who had done very well at Elwood Central, found life at Springvale High very difficult; he couldn't stand any nonsense from his tormentors and would become involved in heated arguments that often led to punch-ups.

It was my first experience of racism in my adopted country, a rude awakening after three years of bliss at Elwood High. I felt lost and lonely. I had been one of the brightest students at Elwood High, but my dream of maintaining academic excellence gradually eroded as a result of the constant racial abuse and innuendo I experienced at Springvale High. I cut my eyelashes and eyebrows. These days that would be called "self-harm", but in those days it just made my mum very cross.

I had worked part-time during school holidays when I was at Elwood High and I continued to do that while at Springvale High. I started as a salesgirl at the Coles Variety Store, on Acland Street, St Kilda, in the bra and briefs department. A few years later, I worked at Myer on the PBA machine (the Permanent Budget Account machine), calculating all the receipts for the day. I had a great desire to earn my own money, and that spurred me on and acted as a counterbalance to what I was experiencing at school.

I decided that the best way to get back at my tormentors was to aim to be publicly successful, so I entered the Miss Springvale contest. I won and, to an extent, that silenced some of my critics. It gave me community connections that I valued, but it also led to boys moving from racism in their taunts to sexual innuendo. And to some even greater concerns at home.

Chapter 4

A ROSE BY ANY OTHER NAME

Our family surname, de Zylva, was the only one in the Melbourne phone book. And, with pictures of me in bikinis being published in *The Age* and *The Sun News-Pictorial*, my name and image was there for any crackpot to view and respond to. Some did – by making obscene phone calls to our family home, some as early as 5am. Our phone was tapped for six months as a way of trying to catch the cranks, and the episode led my father to say that he'd had enough of me entering beauty competitions.

"Can't you change your name?" asked a photographer for the *Sun News Pictorial*, Harry Soeptekauw. He was supportive of my modelling, but I said, "No, I can't. Names are very important in my culture."

But, still, I asked my father whether I could enter the competitions if I took my mother's maiden name. He instantly said no, but then paused, and gave me a little light of hope.

"The only name you could ever take is Pinder," he said, which was my great grandmother's maiden name. My father always said that I reminded him of her so, at age 17, I took that surname and I've had it ever since.

But a new name and the Miss Springvale title didn't help me overcome my troubles at school. The constant barrage of racist taunts drastically affected my studies and I failed my matriculation examination. But I saw that as a wake-up call rather than an opportunity to wallow in self-pity or hit my head against a brick wall in disgust.

I didn't believe then that Australia was a racist country and I don't believe it is now. But, as in most other countries, there are oddballs who indulge in puerile pursuits. Yes, I felt hurt and bullied, and my self-confidence was badly bruised. I empathise with young people today, including sportsmen and sportswomen, who encounter these racist crackpots from time to time.

But I always urge them to do what I did back then. Which was to recognise that the racists were sad people whose malice only displayed their ignorance. They did not speak for the majority of Australians back then, nor do they now. So there was no way I was going to give in to them. I resolved to rise above them, ignore their taunts and join the workforce. This would be the next stage of achieving my dream of making a success of my life.

***

I sat the Federal Public Service test in March 1974 and, when I passed, I requested placement in the Immigration Department. I had also received offers from the Melbourne Metropolitan Board of Works and several banks, but I couldn't see myself as a teller, serving customers, although I was very good at figures. Instead, I had a great desire to explore migration, and especially to be involved in the lives of new migrants, helping them deal with any obstacles they faced.

I had always been unhappy – and remain so – about the White Australia Policy that shrouds the country's past and, with the political winds of change blowing in the 1970s, I was ready to help allay new migrants' fears and convince them Australia was a land of hope.

I soon had that role, assisting many people to attain Australian citizenship while I chatted with them and helped sort out some of their problems. While many of my colleagues were merely interested in getting the job done and going home, I spent a lot of time ensuring that the people I dealt with would not suffer from any official discrimination.

I worked with many migrants whose English was limited and I helped them along during their interviews, making sure they understood their role in Australian society, and the benefits to which they were entitled.

While working with the Immigration Department, I continued to enter and enjoy success in beauty and charity pageants. After I'd won the Miss Springvale contest, I continued to enter them under my new name, Beverley Pinder, always helped along by my mother. She groomed me beautifully and was always willing to buy me lovely clothes and good cosmetics. I've often been asked why I didn't move into modelling, but the truth is I was considered, at five-foot-three, too short and, with my dark hair and skin, too exotic. And I suppose I didn't help my own cause, either: on one of his trips to Australia, the legendary hairdresser Vidal Sassoon wanted to cut my hair, but I said, "No, sorry, it can't be cut!"

Still, the pageants – along with providing great prizes, often for my brothers – continued to build my confidence and self-esteem. I won titles such as Miss Australian Motor Show 1976, along with Miss Glen Waverley Queen of Arts and Victorian Beach Girl. With that success behind me, I was ready in 1978 to pursue what I saw as the holy grail: Miss Universe Australia.

Chapter 5

A PARALLEL UNIVERSE

As I grew up in Ceylon and Australia, I always had that ambition to reach for the stars and wear that shiny princess crown. But this was a whole new level: as the winner of Miss Australian Beauty Queen 1978, I would represent Australia later that year at the Miss Universe contest in Mexico.

Five hundred young Australian women entered the contest, but that number would be whittled down to 35 who would appear at a ceremony in the newly-opened Perth Entertainment Centre. I was thrilled I was chosen to be amongst them, one of five representing Victoria.

I had to travel to Perth alone because my family could not afford the airfares. But I knew as I took to the stage that they would be crowded around the small TV set at home, cheering me on.

It was the first major event held at Perth Entertainment Centre and more than 7,000 people packed the vast hall. At the back were a group of noisy women's libbers, objecting to women being paraded like cattle at a country farm day. Their jeering was loud, but it didn't put me off.

I gasped when my name was announced as a semi-finalist and, to the pulsating rhythm of that catchy Mexican number, 'La Bamba', I danced my way to face the judging panel: *Australian Women's Weekly* editor Ita Buttrose, actor John Waters, ballet legend Sir Robert Helpmann, arts impresario Kym Bonython and former Miss Universe Kerry Wells.

There was a big cheer and roar from the crowd as I stood alongside a gorgeous, curvaceous blue-eyed blonde from Sydney named Susan Wood. Just then I noticed Sue had dropped her bracelet. I picked it up and placed it in her hand and whispered, "Congratulations on being the winner". I genuinely thought I had no hope, but in seconds the master of ceremonies, Jeff Banks, had made the announcement to a hushed audience:

"Ladies and gentlemen, the Australian Beauty Queen, Beverley Pinder!"

The crowd responded with rapturous applause - including the women's libbers, who were cheering for me as the underdog!

The judges' verdict took me by surprise; I didn't think I could win, especially when I was up against a classic blue-eyed blonde. But it had happened. I was Miss Universe Australia 1978, chosen to represent the nation at the Miss Universe contest later in the year in Mexico, along with 80 other beauty queens from around the world.

I'd wanted from a very early age to be a princess and now I definitely was one! The crown on my head was real, a perfect match for the one I'd visualised every night before I'd gone to bed. It was my symbol of success, and now I could very much see that a successful life was taking shape. To me, this was the endorsement I had longed for. Australia was officially accepting me as one of their own.

My family were thrilled when I got home and my colleagues at the Immigration Department were also overwhelmed by my success. The department's bosses arranged for a special photo session so my picture could be taken and sent out on press releases to Australian embassies and consulates around the world. The Liberal Party's Minister for Immigration at the time, Michael Mackellar, even flew down from Canberra to Melbourne to congratulate me.

***

Despite my success, I had no illusions of becoming Miss Universe 1978. I knew I would be up against a bevy of beauties from South America, such as Miss Nicaragua, Miss Peru, Miss Brazil and Miss Colombia, as well as blue-eyed, tall and statuesque blondes from Europe. And then there was the beauty from South Africa considered a favourite, 17-year-old Margaret Gardiner.

As I boarded the Mexico-bound plane, all I was thinking about was gaining positives from what I saw as a unique opportunity. I wanted longevity from the experience of being in this competition. I didn't want the gloss to wear off after a month; I wanted to gain career opportunities from my involvement. That was more important to me than what Miss Universe herself would enjoy during her year-long reign.

Though I received strong coverage from other media, I was taken aback by the Mexican press' reaction to me. In short, they ignored me. Perhaps they were wondering why, as Miss Australia, I didn't have blue eyes and blonde hair.

While the Australian competition had been comparatively friendly, Miss Universe was fraught with intense rivalry. Freneticism and bitchiness behind the scenes – along with a do-or-die mentality – were in abundance. Friends turned on each other, resorting to acts of sabotage and pettiness such as burning and ripping evening gowns, and hiding shoes.

To put it mildly, it was a very interesting four weeks.

Young girls tried to attract photographers so they could have their pictures in the newspapers and perhaps, in some way, influence the judges. Some of them even frolicked in the pool nude, hoping the judges were around.

But we all joined in the program laid out for us, especially at the opening ceremony. With a backdrop of the Convention Centre fountains, the master of ceremonies announced: "And now, live from Acapulco Centre, here are the most beautiful young ladies in the universe!"

We sang a song together in Spanish and English, and as our voices faded in unison, the large audience responded enthusiastically with joyous applause. The stage was set for the parade of beauties that was the Miss Universe Pageant 1978.

***

I found South Africa's Margaret Gardiner to be distinctly different to the other girls. She was very young but had significant experience modelling in Europe, and she maintained her calm demeanour at all times. In Acapulco, all the contestants were accommodated at the luxurious El Camino Real Hotel, and Margaret and I shared a room and became good friends.

There was actually some concern that I had to share a room with a white South African, given her country's apartheid policy at the time. My Australian escorts, Ita Buttrose and Sir Robert Helpmann, were worried I would have problems being with her. But we got on well and, in fact, we were one of the few pairs who shared a room who did not have to be separated due to personality clashes!

I saw Margaret as a winner and decided to help her. She was a beautiful woman in a teenager's body; a chiselled face with bluey-green eyes and a becoming personality. As the final day drew near, I kept her focused on being herself and getting out there and doing what she'd been doing for four weeks. I made sure she was always on time for rehearsals, interviews and photo sessions, and I kept pushing her all the time, giving her much-needed support and motivation.

I didn't realise then that what I was doing for Margaret was probably the true beginning of my later public relations career.

On the day of the big event, contestants had to be out of their rooms by 6 am for rehearsals and photo sessions. We had a short break for lunch and were given sandwiches that one wouldn't feed to a dog. We'd been fed poorly for weeks and I put my foot down and became a spokesperson for the girls. We told organisers we would refuse to do any more work until we were given proper food. My protest created quite a stir, and even Ita Buttrose whispered in my ear to be careful not to cause any problems for the event's organisers.

"You can't form any unions here," she quipped with a smile.

But the girls needed to be fed. We had an exhausting evening schedule that was not going to wind up until midnight. Thankfully, my protest did not fall on deaf ears; we all were given a good meal and treated like human beings.

When Margaret Gardiner was crowned Miss Universe 1978, she was whisked away to another hotel, but she insisted on having breakfast with me in my room the next day. While we were having breakfast, the phone rang. It was Australian broadcaster Derryn Hinch, who had a world-exclusive interview with Margaret. That morning and beyond, she was very loyal to me and grateful for the guidance I gave her. She became in many ways the sister I never had.

While it was an incredible experience, I can't say I enjoyed my time at the Miss Universe contest. It wasn't where I wanted to be. But, still, those four weeks in Mexico gave me confidence for the future and highlighted my tendency to help others and build the profiles and reputations of people who sought my help.

I spent much of the time on the long flight home thinking of what I wanted to do away from the glitz and glamour of beauty pageants. Although I was not Miss Universe, the fact that I, a poor migrant girl from Ceylon, had been crowned Miss Universe Australia was a huge boost to my dreams for the future. But I was not prepared to make a living on the catwalk; I wanted longevity. Sure, I loved the theatre of it, but I also loved interactions with people, particularly the chance to meet important personalities and the networks around them, learning and fostering goodwill.

I realised that I was starting to emerge as a 'people person'.

Chapter 6

WHEN OPPORTUNITY KNOCKS

If there is one thing I've learnt in life that I continue to stand by, it's that you have to look out for the next person, not just yourself. If you do that, the rewards abound. Somewhere, somehow the next person you meet could be your link to a new opportunity.

I realised the opportunity that moving to Australia from Ceylon offered me. And, ever since, I have been good at knowing when opportunity is knocking and have learnt not to be scared to take advantage of those opportunities.

After I arrived back in Melbourne from the Miss Universe contest in Mexico, I was inundated with job offers, but the idea kept recurring to me that I should work in public relations. Hilton Hotels had approached me to be a roving DJ at their Juliana's nightclubs around Australia, but I turned that down. At one stage, I called Geoff Sinclair, organiser of the Miss Universe Australia competition, and asked him what public relations involved. He told me I'd been doing it for myself since I was 14.

"You have already cultivated a terrific relationship with the media," he said. "You have made a name for yourself and you have become a brand in your own right. That's what people do in public relations. And you will be good at it because you are very popular with journalists and photographers, and over the years have gained their trust."

While I was pondering this and my next career move, I received a call from the late Dame Phyllis Frost, who asked me to become involved in a fundraising campaign to upgrade the Maroondah Hospital. She thought a beauty competition – perhaps 'Miss Maroondah' – would be a great way to raise money, and I agreed. We had a few meetings with the hospital's board members and that's when I met Alan Chipp, brother of Don Chipp, the late maverick Senator and founding leader of the Australian Democrats.

Alan was a director of Professional Public Relations (PPR) and his company had applied to do the hospital's public relations work. We got to talking and the "PR" seed really germinated for me. Not long after our conversation, Alan contacted me and said one of his account executives was taking time off to get married and go overseas on her honeymoon. Would I be interested in stepping into her shoes while she was away? I was at the time still working at the Immigration Department, so I took four weeks' annual leave and tried out with Alan's company in March 1979.

***

I learned the ropes while dealing with Stephen Dattner Furs, the late Tony Toumbourou of Travellers Apparel, and a couple of other big accounts. Two weeks into my role, I had organised double-page spreads in *TV Week*, a front page in *The Sun News-Pictorial*, and had done some modelling for Stephen Dattner Furs. When the executive returned from her honeymoon, Alan told her he had hired me to work alongside her. She threw a pencil case at him and stormed angrily out of the room, leaving me with the offer of a full-time position.

I accepted his offer straightaway even though it meant much-reduced remuneration.

I spoke to Vin McHugh, my boss at the Immigration Department, and told him of my decision to resign (not common practice these days when people email or even text their resignations!). He wasn't happy, and even the Minister, Michael Mackellar, contacted me to try to change my mind, saying they had great plans for me. But I reminded them I'd been bitterly disappointed a year earlier when I was rejected for an overseas consular posting. It was time to move on.

I had enjoyed my stint with the Immigration Department because I'd had the opportunity to deal with people on a close and daily basis. It was also where I'd met a tall, blonde, muscular and handsome young man named Richard Norton.

We had noticed each other in the office canteen one day and our relationship had grown from there. Richard was a dedicated martial arts exponent, very determined, and with a positive attitude to life. Martial arts was his first love, so after 11 years with the Immigration Department he quit and became a fully-fledged practitioner. In fact, I trained with him for a while because it complemented my dance skills.

Richard went on to do security work at a popular nightclub and that brought him into contact with a lot of glamorous women. He was soon chosen to provide security for visiting showbiz personalities, including ABBA, Stevie Nicks, The Rolling Stones and Linda Ronstadt. When Ronstadt toured Australia in 1979, Richard and karate instructor Bob Jones were responsible for security. But I had a bad feeling about the tour and sensed my relationship with Richard was on the brink. I had just come back from Mexico after the Miss Universe Contest and Richard seemed uncomfortable that I was always in the spotlight. We had bought a house together in Croydon, but Ronstadt invited him to Los Angeles to be her bodyguard and physical instructor. He left, seeking fame and fortune.

We had been together for little more than five years.

***

With Richard gone, I applied myself fully to my new career with Alan Chipp's PPR.

The office was a small West Melbourne terrace house, and Chipp co-managed it with Harry Smith, the former finance editor at *The Sun.* Alan handled the marketing clients, while Harry took care of the business and finance clients. The other two staff members were our copywriter, and me.

Harry and Alan were very talented, so I watched them and learned from them. With exacting attention to detail, Harry crunched PPR's numbers, while Alan never settled for second best and was demanding and unforgiving. If I had got a page one for Stephen Dattner Furs on Monday and rival leather clothing specialist Eric Planinsek had page three on Thursday, Alan would be upset with me, arguing I should have aimed for page three on Thursday for Stephen Dattner as well.

Stephen Dattner, larger than life and a man I considered the ultimate marketeer, was my main client, and he was quite content with the publicity I generated for his furs. He knew his customers well and understood their behaviour. And I learnt a lot from this gentle giant, including that any idea is a good one, and if ever you faltered he would expect you to pick yourself up and have another go.

I quickly became accustomed to attending meetings and setting agendas, becoming proactive about getting the maximum publicity for the account. I did not restrict my energies to getting Dattner fashion spreads, but had his company involved in *pro-bono* work as well, such as an annual Christmas party for underprivileged children.

Because Dattner only had a Melbourne outlet, I also assisted him by arranging a roadshow, taking Dattner Furs around Australia. I even had him ride a camel from Melbourne to Sydney, launching the successful and fun campaign on Channel Nine's *Good Morning Australia,* hosted by Kerri-Anne Kennerley.

Even if it was a public holiday, I was always there for my clients because I treated PPR as if it were my own business. That's how passionate I was about my new career. The picture editors of *The Herald* and *The Sun* were delighted with my pictorial concepts because it made their job of looking for good newspaper spreads so much easier. I had a beautiful, bikini-clad model photographed in a Dattner fur at high noon on St Kilda Beach, and had sand dunes at Clayton converted into artificial ski slopes.

I introduced new clients to PPR, such as Courtaulds Hilton, known for its famous Hilton and Kayser lingerie, and I handled PPR's high-profile retailer David Wang Emporium. One morning, Mrs Wang called me to attend a meeting at her office where she told me that the Wang Emporium was closing down and she had plans to lease the building. She wanted PPR to go with the announcement. It was an unusual request, and I promised to think about it. But Mrs Wang was adamant.

"The man from London who wants to lease the building wants PR."

This "man from London" was Richard Branson. He wasn't a "Sir" in those days, just a businessman looking to kickstart his Virgin Records Australia operations by launching the country's first Virgin Megastore in Melbourne.

I came up with the idea that Richard Branson, who would one day promise to take people on rides into space, should ride an elephant from the steps of State Parliament down Bourke Street to the Wang Emporium building. Mrs Wang loved the idea – and so did Branson.

I managed to have Bourke Street closed down for two hours for the event, and the media had a field day covering the grand entrance of little-known, hippy-looking Richard Branson astride an elephant, which I'd hired from my circus friends, the Perry Brothers.

Ever the adventurer, Branson rode the elephant into the Wang Emporium building, breaking a few of Mrs Wang's expensive porcelain items in the shop. Thankfully, nothing else untoward happened; I was very worried the elephant would poop up and down Bourke Street and leave PPR with a huge cleaning bill. But we did miss a golden opportunity: we should have signed Sir Richard Branson as a client when his career was just starting to take off.

***

While my career was building at PPR in 1979, I met a handsome, blue-eyed photographer from *The Sun* named Peter Cox. He was assigned to do a photoshoot at the Moonee Valley Racecourse during which I was supposed to stand and be photographed with the Colin Hayes-trained winning horse. But this upstart photographer asked me to stand aside while he took a picture of the horse with the trainer. Unperturbed, I stepped aside – and vowed I would square with him one day.

He did it again when I arranged a photoshoot for a Persian carpet client. I went to great lengths to promote the concept of model Gail Page dressed in a harem outfit, like TV's lovable Barbara Eden from *I Dream of Jeannie,* on a magic flying carpet. The concept meant a lot of hard work, involving securing the magic carpet with fish wire. But Coxy snubbed me and instead took the model aside, rolled up the carpet, put it on her shoulder and took her picture, totally ignoring my concept.

Enough was enough – I took up the challenge!

I invited him to PPR's Christmas party that year, we got to know each other better, and I ended up marrying him in 1983.

***

Three years into working with PPR, I was interested in becoming a partner in the business. It was the '80s and women were just emerging into management roles, and I was confident I could move to the next level of my career. Realising that it might be a stretch for Alan to consider me as a partner, I asked him whether we might start an offshoot with me in charge and in which he and Harry would have a financial interest. Alan strung me along for three years, promising to discuss my proposal with his partner. Finally, in 1985, he told me that Harry didn't think there was a role for a female in management.

They didn't explicitly say so, but I got the feeling that they didn't think that a female should be treated as an equal partner in their business, despite the work I had put in, and the value I had added to their business.

I'd hit the infamous 'glass ceiling' women often encountered in the workforce back then. It still exists today, of course. It may be a hurdle, but it should not be a barrier that women can't get past. I was determined not to let it stop my career from progressing.

There was no time for tears of regret and sorrow. While it was bitterly disappointing, because I'd generated a lot of business for PPR in six and a half years, I wasn't going to meekly accept this knockback. I handed in my resignation the next day.

I came home and told Coxy about my resignation, but he didn't seem anxious about the situation. Instead, he picked up his jacket and made for the door, saying he was going to look for an office.

"An office?" I pleaded, confused.

"Yes, so you can start your own business."

He found me a serviced apartment in a block on Queens Road, now the Pullman Melbourne Albert Park. It was a first-floor, one-room flat with a small kitchen. Coxy hung a few pictures he'd enlarged of some projects I'd handled. We transformed the place into a cosy little office, waiting to burst into life. He also arranged a secretarial service to handle all my typing.

On Saturday 1 June, 1985, we set up the place to start business on the Monday. Then, on Sunday, we called on Father Ernie Smith, founder of Sacred Heart Mission. He opened the doors three nights a week to alcoholics, drug addicts and prostitutes who wanted a listening ear, some food and a cuppa. That afternoon I wore my Stephen Dattner racoon fur coat and left it in our car, parked in Grey St, St Kilda, with my handbag and precious book of contacts. We finished our meeting with Father Ernie and returned to our car about two hours later to find the windows shattered and my fur coat and handbag gone.

I was speechless and wondered if this was a bad omen for our future plans. I didn't mind losing the coat and the handbag, but that contact book was irreplaceable. We drove around for two hours, searching St Kilda's labyrinthine streets, hoping to find my stolen handbag, but to no avail. We reported the theft at the police station then returned home, depressed and exhausted. The phone rang at 11.00 pm: the police had found my handbag – it was empty except for my green contact book and a little book of Catholic novena prayers I had brought with me from Ceylon. I was so relieved. And my bad omen disappeared, replaced by a more positive outlook.

I drove into the carpark of my new office complex at 7.30 am the next day, clueless about what to do on this first day of the rest of my life. Then the phone rang at 9.15 am: John Mitchell, a photographer from *The Sun* newspaper, who said he'd tried to reach me at PPR to respond to an invitation I'd sent him on behalf of Nicholas Dattner. Later, Nicholas Dattner called, confused about why he couldn't reach me at PPR.

"What the f#*% are you doing?" he asked. "You're *my* f#*%ing PR consultant."

I pleaded with Nicholas that I could not look after his account any longer because it belonged to PPR. But he wouldn't take no for an answer. He hung up and rang me two hours later.

"Well, you better get cracking," he said. "I told Alan exactly what I thought of him and the account is now yours."

By the third week, my confidence was sky high. I saw an advertisement in the morning newspaper about Westfield celebrating its 25th anniversary so I phoned the marketing manager, Fran Morris. I had met her once at the Greensborough Shopping Centre; and I suggested we talk about working out a PR arrangement between Westfield and my company. Fran was very keen to promote Westfield shopping centres at Southland, Airport West and Doncaster; and I went to her with a raft of promotion ideas. She signed me up without hesitation and Westfield became my first retainer client and one of my best.

Westfield had always been dear to me because I won Junior Miss Victoria at Doncaster Shoppingtown. And, with that one client, I was earning more than I had at PPR. I had four clients by week three, which I viewed as an amazing achievement, and the revenue generated was at least five times as much as I had previously earned in one year.

More business came my way, this time the main Dattner account. I bid for the contract – presumably with PPR also making a bid – when it came up for renewal and was successful. Around this time, however, Stephen Dattner was looking for a successor, and his daughter, Fabian, was being groomed for the role of managing director. Stephen called me aside and asked me to help his "hippie daughter from Eltham" to build her profile and management persona to enable her to manage the business after he stepped down. I gladly did, and she was great to work with.

Fabian soon developed a media cult following. I admired her honesty, tenacity, strong will and willingness to give anything a go. Above all, she had a heart of gold; and she continued to bring the second-to-none family values to the Dattner business.

With my clientele increasing, including big accounts such as Pelaco, Tupperware, Mothercare, Hang Ten and Watersun and Ada swimwear, I needed a bigger office, so we moved to a two-room apartment in the same complex a year later in 1988.

Soon after, however, my business success was tempered by sad family news that would lead to a complete personal upheaval.

Chapter 7

RELATIONSHIP TURMOIL

Coxy's father Daryl died on 17 November 1985 and this sad event coincided with the first signs of cracks in our marriage. Although I'd got along well with Daryl, I'd never been accepted as a member of his family. When the funeral notice appeared in the newspapers, my name was left out. I expected Coxy to take issue with his family over this, but he didn't offer a whimper and I was saddened by this weakness on Coxy's part.

I was working up to 20 hours a day, grabbing a few hours of sleep when I could, and this disenfranchisement from Coxy's family was too much to handle.

My days started at 5.30 am and I didn't get home until well after midnight. There were no computers in that era, so I handwrote reams of copy for my secretarial service to type up the next day. I soldiered on with the workload because the increasing number of clients was also offering me great satisfaction and I was able to *buy* a larger office; a single-level premises in Port Melbourne with a boardroom, conference room, large kitchen, and street exposure of my business signage: *Beverley Pinder Public Relations.*

But the stress of managing the business began to take its toll. I developed a rash on my hands and feet and had to wear white cotton gloves and socks to work. I abandoned my wardrobe of beautiful outfits and wore clothes that wouldn't pull on my skin. And my marriage to Coxy was on the brink, and soon became untenable.

When I decided to leave Coxy in August 1991, we agreed to negotiate the terms of settlement directly, without involving any lawyers. My top priority was to retain my business, in which Coxy had become co-director. In order to buy him out, I had to sacrifice some of my property investments. I also had to sell the premises of the Port Melbourne office at a fire-sale rate.

After the divorce settlement, I had no choice but to downsize; I leased office space in Park Street, South Melbourne, and reduced my staff from six to one. All this coincided with the 1991 recession that then Treasurer Paul Keating told us we had to have. But I still had strength and enthusiasm and wasn't ready to throw in the towel. And as often happens, opportunity knocked when the chips were down.

I found that Rowland Australia, another Melbourne public relations firm, was suffering. I contacted Sean Barrett, Rowland Australia's boss, and asked if I could buy the Rowland name for my business.

"*Buy?* No, we will give it to you," was his instant response. The only condition was that I had to maintain the Rowland name in Melbourne along with my name. So, without any money changing hands, I took on Melbourne's Rowland franchise and became Rowland Pinder Public Relations in August 1993.

Rowland in Melbourne had only three clients left: MMI Insurance (now Allianz Insurance), Tourism Authority of Thailand and Elgas. I salvaged MMI Insurance from the jaws of death, turned it around with help from the company's marketing director and maintained the account for many years.

Even though there was no work forthcoming from Rowland's international base, I used the name to widen the scope of the service I could provide prospective clients nationally and internationally. Opportunity kept knocking, and I kept answering

***

About this time, I was at a social function when I was introduced to corporate giant Solomon Lew, head of the Coles-Myer empire, at the time. He deeply distrusted journalists and shunned them whenever possible. He believed journalists wrote whatever they wanted, taking scant interest in facts and basing their stories on misinformation.

I put it to him that if he didn't communicate with journalists and instead kept crying foul over so-called "misinformation", how could journalists ever write correct and balanced stories about him and his business?

In my early days working in PR, I was at the newspaper offices at 2.00 am, reading the papers as they rolled off the presses. I'd always known that if journalists wrote stories without input from you, all hell could break loose. That's why over many years I'd built up good relationships with journos.

After my informal chat with Mr Lew about the media, his PA put a call in to my office asking if I was available to meet with the Coles-Myer chief. I thought my receptionist was joking at first. But, no, could I meet with him tomorrow?

Talk about opportunity knocking!

My meeting with Solomon Lew was an unforgettable experience. His office was on the 51st floor of 101 Collins Street and had recently been refurbished. As I entered the inner sanctum of the boardroom, I stood breathless, surveying the scene: a large polished table with a mirror-like surface, comfortable leather chairs around it, and imposing modern abstract paintings on the walls. The fabulous environment left me awestruck.

I was wearing an expensive black Louis Feraud suit, hoping to impress. I scanned the room and caught sight of the great man himself, his eyes in turn watching me with close scrutiny. He was impeccably dressed in a well-tailored dark suit and as he extended his right hand to shake mine, I noticed how beautifully manicured his nails were, with a hint of clear varnish. Very politely, he ushered me to a round side table and spoke about the forthcoming Coles-Myer AGM. He wanted me to head off a possible onslaught by his nemesis, shareholder activist Jack Gruzmann, who habitually caused mayhem at such corporate events. I did this by placing Solomon Lew in the media spotlight, where he'd never been, which took some of the shine away from Gruzmann and his media-monopolising tactics. In time, I was able to help Lew become comfortable with greater media exposure, gradually eliminating his distrust of journalists.

Solomon Lew was very punctual and expected others to show him the same courtesy. As Coles-Myer chairman, he took it upon himself to visit every Australian Coles store at least once a year. He was very thorough in his business ways and no one could pull the proverbial wool over his eyes. He was a creator, a man with a persona that epitomised momentum, a man always on the go.

In the five months I worked with him (September '93 to January '94), I built a great respect for Solomon Lew and the charisma he exuded as a captain of industry. And I always felt he was not revered highly enough, in the 90s, by the corporate world and the media. I made myself available whenever he called – being a practical joker he usually identified himself on the phone as 'Billy Bunter' or another cartoon character – and never missed charity events he sponsored with his then wife, Rosie.

He had impeccable dress sense and I was always conscious of how neat and tidy he wanted the environments he was in to be. So, giving him a ride in my BMW one day, he was appalled at how dirty it was, inside and out.

"If you work for me, there is no way I will give you a car," he said.

"If I work for you and you give me a car, I will have someone clean it every week," I laughed.

My five months working with Solomon Lew were very rewarding, yet challenging, as I helped him navigate his media affairs. The day I left him, however, he held my hand and acknowledged that I had given him the ability to trust journalists.

But Solomon Lew wasn't the only captain of industry with whom I worked, and from whom I learnt so much.

***

Tony D'Aloisio is another corporate icon with a similar vision to Solomon Lew's. I met him when my company handled the account for the law firm Mallesons Stephen Jaques (now King and Wood Mallesons), of which he was Chief Executive Partner. D'Aloisio, who was head of ASIC until 2011, following his days at the helm of Mallesons Stephen Jaques, has an amazing mind, one of the finest I have worked with. A hard taskmaster who was demanding and unforgiving, he was not for the faint-hearted, but it was a real privilege to have worked with him.

There was also a man I met in 1993 at, of all places, a seminar called "Women for all Seasons". There were 18 women and two men at the seminar, which opened with a barn dance! We swapped partners and I found myself dancing with one of the two men, who introduced himself as David Bardas. The penny dropped as to why he was one of the two men here: Bardas was then at the helm of the Sportsgirl/Sportscraft Group, one of Australia's greatest fashion retailing enterprises.

Bardas was known in the industry as a powerful advocate for empowering women. During his time at Sportsgirl, the glass ceiling was shattered before its presence was even recognised elsewhere. He had a strong desire for action and would become frustrated when malaise clouded his vision of progress. My kind of man, indeed.

He contested as an independent for Melbourne City Council in

1996 with the slogan 'David Bardas – the Passionate Candidate'. He was elected and got moving on his vision to make Melbourne a "more exciting place to live, work, shop and play". I was his campaign manager and I worked hard to get his message across. But this passionate man was soon confronted by inaction of the Council. He resigned after two and a half years in what he described as "disappointment, frustration, disillusionment and concern" that the democratically-elected Council wasn't working in the best interests of the city.

In 2000, Bardas published *Clown Hall – An Insider's Guide to Bureaucracy*, which revealed the local government system's deficiencies, particularly Melbourne City Council's problems. What he found most frustrating was "elected Councillors not in control of policy, with a bureaucracy with its own agenda"'. He believed in "grassroots, bottom-up democracy where people feel part of the system – where they don't feel thwarted, alienated and frustrated by the bureaucratic process". And he had this advice for politicians at all levels of government: "Keep your election promises. Remember you, not the bureaucrats, were elected to make decisions . . ."

Sadly, they are words that continue to fall on deaf ears in governments everywhere.

***

My business was booming and, at 36, I was professionally happy. But, after my divorce from Peter Cox, I was missing the company of a partner. That was when I met Paul Sadler, who was 45 and a wealthy businessman who enjoyed maintaining his fitness, and keeping some structure in his routine, by working as a swimming instructor.

Paul was very much the larrikin and reminded me a little of my father, exuding a certain charm which women found attractive. And our relationship made me more aware of myself and my fragility; we all need someone to expose ourselves to. That was one of Paul's redeeming features; he was good at leading people to look at themselves closely.

Having led a stable and secure life with Coxy, I found it difficult, however, to put up with Paul's distractions. Committed only to his swimming instruction, he had a lot of time on his hands, while I was busy with my business and embarking on new horizons. I was enjoying a dream run with new accounts, but he was enjoying his free time cycling, going on his long walks and lunching with attractive women.

I tried to end our rocky relationship of seven years many times by walking out; I was pretty much his doormat. But one day, after I had left him for the seventh time, he proposed marriage and he won me over. Paul had the gift of the 'charismatic gab', which people found very persuasive.

***

A civil celebrant married us in March 1996 at a private ceremony for 50 guests. My mother and three brothers, Errol, Durand and Dillon, were there, but Sandy refused to come. He was disappointed because I'd signed a pre-nuptial agreement that I wouldn't bear any children. Paul didn't want any; he'd been married previously and had a son by that marriage.

I had selected Celine Dion's *Power of Love* as our wedding's theme song. I realise now the words defined love as not only being about what someone else could give you, but what you offered yourself. Still, it was a joyous occasion and we left on our overseas honeymoon, a gift to Paul because he'd nurtured a dream to see the Taj Mahal, in Agra, India. We also had France, Italy and Monaco on our itinerary. I wanted him to enjoy the trip because he had before that only been to Bali.

Paul bought me a handmade marble centrepiece in Agra, but it cracked to smithereens. I am generally not superstitious, but that was a bad omen because the honeymoon wasn't exactly the romantic getaway I had hoped for. The two-week trip was often soured by Paul's larrikinism; he tended to look down on other cultures and was often quite vocal about it. I was deeply offended by his attitude and we had constant arguments about it.

I was relieved when we returned to Australia, because the stress was getting to me. Was it a honeymoon to remember? Yes, but for the wrong reasons.

After a mere three months of married life, I knew I wanted to call it quits. I realised that Paul wanted me as a 'trophy wife' and couldn't understand why I did not do what the glamour set did: cosmetic surgery, facials, painted nails and the like. But I'd left all that behind when I walked away from the bright lights of my Miss Australia days.

I decided to see a psychologist to sort myself out. After counselling, I stayed with Paul for another 18 months, but our relationship only got worse. We argued constantly and things got physical on a couple of occasions. That was it for me, I walked out. I later learnt that Paul's first marriage had lasted just 18 months.

***

I rented a one-bedroom flat in Beaconsfield Parade and wasn't coping well; the failed marriage had taken everything out of me. Stress caused the rash to reappear on my hands, and I also suffered a business setback when one of my prized clients, Mallesons, pulled out. They were happy with my service, but after their merger with Stephen Jaques Stone James, they wanted in-house public relations.

I was at the lowest point in my life and I even contemplated suicide by gassing myself in my car.

I called my lawyer first, to brief him on a few matters I needed him

Beverley, far right, aged 8, with her cousins in Ceylon.

Beverley, second from left, at her maternal grandma's 60th, with her uncle Bert and aunty Tazma (far left), very early role models.

Beverley after winning the 14-16 years' section in the Junior Miss Victoria 1971.

Beverley, aged 15, ready for her first gala dance.

Beverley, third row, first of the three roses amongst the boys.

Springvale High School friend, Persefoni (left) and Beverley aged 21 in Hawaii.

Beverley, at 15, takes a dip at Edithvale Beach – photo taken by John Lamb.

Beverley and her dad at home in Springvale – two days after winning the 1978 Australian Beauty Queen title in Perth

Watching Miss Colombia at Miss Universe, 1978.

Beverley and her roommate and Miss Universe 1978, Margaret Gardiner, at Healesville Sanctuary, 1

Parading down the streets of Mexico.

Beverley at the City of Melbourne's Free Entertainment in the Park program modelling a Jenny Banister creation.

Beverley the bureaucrat meets Beverley the beauty queen meets Beverley the PR superstar, Beverley and Immigration Minister Michael McKellar in 1978.

Beverley and Rhia modelling works of hair art by Alfred Santo in 1976.

to attend to, but he kept me talking for more than an hour because he realised what I was planning to do. In doing so, he fortunately talked me out of it. I am very grateful for that second chance.

That experience taught me never to panic when the chips are down. Nowadays, if I'm under huge stress, I pull back and paint a very big picture in my head. I then start dividing it into sections, dealing with one section at a time. In the same way I 'chunk' my workload, I 'chunk' personal crises. I find that a lot easier than trying to deal with the whole problem head-on.

I never look at a crisis now as something too difficult to handle. I try to build a border around it to contain it, otherwise it could spread and become the big problem I fear it to be. And, often, it is only *fear* that we're talking about; fear of what might happen, rather than what is actually going on.

I sit calmly and think through the issue on my own. I keep the tears away and never think of the consequences or 'why me?' at this time. If I did, I'd only wallow in self-pity. When I am alone dealing with a problem, I write down my thoughts because I think it's easier to find a solution when thoughts are recorded. And I never let animosity creep in; it's hard to move forward if you're still in that state.

Next, I work out who I need to bounce it off. We need good listeners for our problems, but not people who are totally sympathetic. Listeners have to be rational and not cloud issues with their sympathy. My family thinks I am too harsh when I deal with their problems, but that's me; I don't believe in giving anyone false hope with sympathy.

If I don't have anyone who is a rational listener, I sit in front of a mirror and talk to myself. At some stage I find I am analysing myself. To me, that is part of the recovery process that helps ensure such a situation never happens again.

My psychologist also helped me immensely, and I believe people involved in managing a business should always consider using one. They are as important as financial advisers, mentors and coaches. I had one psychologist, Adele Borge, from the time I developed a skin condition. The dermatologist who treated me said he could fix the skin condition, but I needed to fix myself as well – and for that I would need a psychologist. I saw Adele up until she retired. She was an excellent 'sounding board' and helped me through times of extreme pressure.

In the end, I can see that my approach to dealing with personal crises has a lot in common with how I deal with clients' professional needs. I take time to look at each aspect of a client's problem, knowing I can add value to two-thirds of the problem, but sometimes the other third is hard to resolve. I acknowledge that to my clients, but constantly place on the agenda how the rest of the problem should be tackled. We always work together to quash the problem or perhaps recognise that we might need further assistance. Collaboration is vital in such situations. A problem shared is a problem halved.

After the stress of feeling suicidal and finally getting back on my feet, I found I could move forward. Despite two failed marriages, I had a business to manage; and I had to pick up the pieces of my personal life and make a fresh start. I bought a two-bedroom apartment and office space in an adjacent building in Albert Road, South Melbourne. But, despite resettling and trying to get some order back into my life, I was about to encounter more drama.

Chapter 8

SECOND CHANCE

Working with Fabian Dattner, I had teamed up with her on a project she called 'Second Chance', which involved providing former prisoners work opportunities. The project began when Fabian personally gave an ex-offender a second chance.

Furs were stolen from the Dattner warehouse in Clifton Hill one evening. In an interview the next day that I had organised for her with legendary radio host Michael Schildberger, Fabian threw out a challenge to the thief.

"I would love the bloke who stole my furs last night to talk to me about it."

Later in the day, her phone rang. The fur-thief said he'd done it because he was just out of jail and needed money. And, more importantly he said, he needed a job.

Fabian hired him on the spot as a cleaner.

Her gesture caught on and the hugely successful Second Chance was born in the late 1980s. Many major businesses gave their support, along with the State Government. A year into the program, Fabian and I took 15 CEOs to Pentridge and sat them in a room with 20 prisoners. With Fabian moderating, together, they came up with more than 200 ideas about how to encourage and motivate prisoners once they were released.

My involvement with this program was very much on my mind when I agreed to attach myself to a venture to lease Sale Prison as a bail centre. The aim was to alleviate the overcrowding problem in Victorian prisons and the pitch was based on saving the State Government money while easing the workload and stress of the overworked prison staff.

The idea came from a recently-paroled prisoner – let's call him Greg, who had befriended my brother Errol 'inside'. Errol had become ensnared in the drug world, and was serving time for drug trafficking. So when Greg approached me (with Errol's ok) to discuss this idea, I was willing to listen, to consider its merits, and perhaps to help.

After my commitment to Second Chance, I didn't have a problem with associating with ex-offenders. Fabian and I had always believed that those who had done time and paid their debt to society deserved that second chance. I had even given Greg a key to my office and access to a computer, while always making it clear our relationship had to be based on honesty and transparency.

With some useful PR tactics, I made sure, however, that the public received the right message about the project.

As the venture got moving, I was mooted as a potential chairperson. I was in the process of making a careful study of the plan when Greg prematurely released information to the State Government, jumping the gun to use my name as chairperson. The *Sunday Herald Sun* got wind of Greg's criminal past, and all hell broke loose : Beverley Pinder, former beauty queen, was mixing with criminal elements!

With some useful PR tactics, I made sure, however, that the public received the right message about the project.

My trusted journalist friend at the *Herald Sun*, Geoff Wilkinson, interviewed me for a story. He was briefed on how Greg came to contact me. I told Geoff the truth, how I believed in the bail centre project, and reminded him of my involvement in Second Chance. I didn't disown my brother, I said that he had become a model prisoner, and I was confident he would learn from his mistakes rather than repeat them.

Geoff's April 1998 story told of a company that Greg had created, which operated a halfway house for released prisoners. I also explained in the article that I had not made a firm commitment because I was in the process of talking to my lawyer and making sure all bases were covered before I made my decision on having any involvement with the bail centre. Becoming involved in such a project could obviously convey the wrong message to the public, so I had to avoid that and win its support.

Geoff quoted me as saying: "I am interested in drug rehabilitation for released offenders, but I am not interested in getting involved in anything which is open to question or innuendo."

After the *Herald Sun* story, however, the Kennett government, originally keen on implementing the project, pulled out.

Thankfully, the fallout for me was minimal. Many prominent people, such as country and western singing idol Johnny Chester and entrepreneur, the late Brian Goldsmith, offered me support. People whose lives I had touched, even briefly, were also protecting my reputation. I put it all down to my belief in being honest and briefing journalists accurately. It's why I abhor the 'spin doctor' tagline associated with the public relations profession. *Of course*, I did put a positive spin on the products and services I promote for clients, but I never lie about them.

I sent letters to my clients explaining my role in the sad episode; that I had loaned my name and support to a proposed non-profit venture which, unfortunately, took a turn for the worse. I did not have a single negative response from them.

The episode was a major distraction, but I never shifted my focus from my business. My public relations skills, as well as my mother's tenacity to ride tough times and my late father's often genteel qualities, helped me weather the storm.

***

It was 1998 and I was about to enter my 20th year in business. It was very profitable, but the workload was becoming too great and I knew I had to seriously consider whether I could manage any further growth. I had always toyed with employing more staff and expanding, but I also wanted to preserve the ability to be involved closely with each client. Quality control was paramount; work not only had to get done, it had to get done properly.

I knew a partnership would help me take the next step. I tried to attract one and had discussions with major companies, including international businesses. Nearly all, however, wanted me and my clients, but not my staff. And they wanted to know how many contracts I had with clients. That was a difficult question to answer because I have never favoured contracts. If a client didn't want to work with me, I'd much rather say, "Thank you so much, it was great being with you" and walk away. And, if my staff couldn't be part of the deal, my loyalty to them meant I had to say no to potential partners. It didn't matter to me if a staff member had been with me for two weeks or two years, I remained loyal.

I have always kept my business at a moderate size, which has allowed me to have a close rapport with staff and clients. Throughout my career, this has also allowed me to continue to have personal – and business – involvement in my other great passion: charity work.

Chapter 9

CHARITY IS IN MY DNA

From my first ventures into raising funds for charity as a beauty pageant entrant, to working with Fabian Dattner on Second Chance, charity work has been a powerful motivating force in my life and business. It stemmed from my belief that, as an immigrant, I had come to a 'land of milk and honey', yet some children and young people here were underprivileged, particularly in Aboriginal communities. So I became involved with various charities organised by, among others, Lions Club and Yooralla.

In 1991, I joined a group of businessmen and women who met monthly to assist chosen charities to develop workable models and business networks. The group, which I was part of for three years, included finance, marketing, manufacturing and public relations experts, among others.

Soon after, I became involved with 'Caring' which I helped re-brand as 'Crisis Line'. I joined the committee and found the board lacking in robust personalities able to introduce new thinking and contacts. During five years with Crisis Line, I brought in a range of people with special skills to help the organisation become dynamic and relevant.

My next charity work came about in 1995 when David Bardas introduced me to the non-profit Gawler Foundation. David was then president of the organisation, founded by cancer survivor Dr Ian Gawler, which helped people affected by serious illnesses, such as cancer and multiple sclerosis. Based in the Yarra Valley, many volunteers professionally managed and supported the Foundation, including a volunteer board. David was then looking for someone to raise the Foundation's profile and I volunteered, doing my bit to attract the right publicity. I was a board member and vice-president until March 2007.

In February 2005, Karin Knoester joined the Foundation as CEO. When she was appointed, we discovered the organisation was severely in the red and only weeks away from going under. I worked with Karin and Ian Gawler, helping pull the organisation back from the brink over a period of 18 months.

My work with not-for-profits continued and two very special charities that I became involved in were the Father Bob Maguire Foundation and the Lighthouse Foundation.

Both charities had at the helm two very special people whom I held in high regard, and whose work I was committed to supporting.

My work with the late Father Bob involved introducing him to potential donors and supporters who could help get his Commons project off the ground. In case there are any readers who don't know who Father Bob was, he was the parish priest at St Peter's and St Paul's Church in South Melbourne, from 1973-2012. One of his initiatives was to establish the South Melbourne Commons, on a Church-owned property next to St Peter's and St Paul's, as a community hub including a communal garden, a sensory garden, a bicycle workshop and various children's activities.

He was made a Member of the Order of Australia in 1989, for services to homeless youth through the Open Family Foundation.

The Father Bob Maguire Foundation was established in 2003, to bring his various social welfare initiatives under one board of governance.

After the Church authorities obliged him to retire as parish priest in 2012, Father Bob focused on his charitable projects full-time. Undeterred by the Church administrators' decision not to renew the Commons' lease on its original site, he negotiated the use of a warehouse in Gladstone St, South Melbourne, and invited the Commons' management to continue operating there.

Like many in the community, I felt drawn to support his Foundation by Father Bob's blunt but colorful personality, his absence of pretence and self-interest, and his genuine concern for the less-fortunate members of our community.

Susan Barton AM established the Lighthouse Foundation in 1991. Its purpose is to provide homes and therapeutic care for children who are homeless, or whose lives have been affected by homelessness, neglect or abuse.

Susan could see that I had a lot to offer the Fundraising Committee in the way of ideas and my own skills in PR.

They were days of abundance in the corporate sector, yet to get a charity to understand sustainability and striving to reach a point where the charity can afford to pay its rent, its people and undertake the work it does - was almost impossible.

Still to this day, the charity dollar is hard to come by - especially when you find that climate change, mental health, domestic and sexual violence, and care for our children have emerged as key issues which tend to receive support and donations ahead of organisations whose purpose is charity *per se*.

My pro bono efforts continue to this day and while in semi-retirement, my only real work becomes the issues that others have to solve with little or no budgets nor wherewithal on how to navigate the plethora of government and corporate requirements to facilitate applications for donor support.

During my days as a City of Melbourne Councillor, I got to know Major Brendan Nottle and his work at the Salvation Army's Project 614. We often engage in brainstorming ideas to help the vulnerable or those experiencing homelessness. One such program is the Pink Car initiative which operates overnight on Fridays and Saturdays across the city and inner city, including City of Melbourne and City of Stonnington, helping to ensure that young women can get home safely after enjoying some of Melbourne's late-night activities.

While the Pink Car is being heavily supported by the Collingwood Football Club and the Office of Women, I arranged funding for the maintenance of the car over 12 months, with a young Sri Lankan-born entrepreneur Rocket Ilukpitiya, CEO of Cloudmarc.

In the early 2000s, I was keen to launch a charity called 'What A Difference a Day Makes'. The idea behind this was to motivate people to donate a day of their time each year – 24 hours in 365 days – to help a charity do its work. Other commitments intervened, and I did not get that idea off the ground. But I still maintain, if you can give your time, this is very precious. Whether it is on a board, helping promote the great work of the charity, selling tickets to a fundraising event, donating personal funds, or even approaching your friends and contacts for giveaways for Raffles and prizes, it all helps.

***

Perhaps the biggest single fund-raising project I have been involved with was prompted by the widespread devastation brought to my former homeland, Sri Lanka, by the Boxing Day Tsunami in 2004.

I was taking a break at my retreat in Portsea when my old friend, Australia's first celebrity chef, Peter Russell-Clarke, phoned and gave me the horrifying news.

I wasn't watching television at the time and I was dumbstruck when he spoke to me. I felt useless. My first instinct was to get on a plane and go to Sri Lanka, but then I thought I'm not a doctor, nurse or psychologist; I would simply be in the way of those involved in the massive rescue efforts.

I was in tears the next day when David Bardas dropped in. He suggested I dry my tears and swing into action by emailing everyone I knew who had Sri Lankan friends and might help out. I contacted

HELP Sri Lanka Inc., an organisation that a group of Victorian Sri Lankans had formed, and offered to raise funds to help those the devastation had affected.

I introduced Melbourne City Council's Susan Riley to HELP Sri Lanka, and took her to Sri Lanka four months after the tsunami so she could see the devastation first-hand. We covered almost 2,000 km in five days, travelling to Trincomalee, Batticaloa and surrounding areas. Susan was later nominated a patron of HELP Sri Lanka.

A major donation of $100,000 from the Sri Lanka Association of Victoria (SLAV) enabled HELP to make a significant contribution towards a City of Melbourne project. It involved the construction of two new levels at the North Dickwella School in south Sri Lanka. Twelve schools in the area had been destroyed, so North Dickwella saw its student numbers rise suddenly from 300 to 1,200.

I was able to get help from three Victorian schools: Gladstone Park Secondary College, Craigieburn South Primary and Greenvale Primary. Together, they donated $9,000 for a new science lab at North Dickwella. I also negotiated with England's prestigious King's College to have them provide a modern kitchen for the school and an ongoing nutrition program. King's College made an initial donation of $2,500, with more money forwarded as the fundraising program kicked in.

In March 2007, I travelled to Sri Lanka with a delegation from SLAV and HELP Sri Lanka for the opening of the school's new wing. North Dickwella's Principal, Rev. Dhammavilasa Thero, said, "We can now offer science subjects to our students and prepare them for Advanced Level classes. This is a very happy occasion. This is a school located in the rural corner of Sri Lanka offering education to children of poor communities . . . We can now embark on a brave and exciting journey to upgrade this school as a centre of excellence in Matara, giving new hope and a bright future for our children."

There were tears in my eyes when I spoke to some of the excited young students in their spotless white uniforms. One girl, barely 10, looked at the equipment in the new science lab and said in Sinhalese: "Now I will be able to become a doctor when I am big."

Talking to her brought back memories of my student days in Kirillapona in the early '60s and my own dreams of what I could become in the future.

Mother Teresa said, "Give till it hurts." I have tried to put no boundaries on generosity. I have done a lot of charity work and will continue to do so.

My late mother often warned me "that's enough" when it came to giving to others. But I knew what it was to struggle, so if the opportunity ever presents itself, I want to do all I can to help others in need. And, in my business life and elsewhere, that has especially included helping women to be all they can be.

Chapter 10

SPEAKING OF CHARITY

When it comes to charity. I have always drawn inspiration form the late Mother Teresa (now officially Saint Teresa of Calcutta), the Catholic nun who spent her life caring for the destitute and dying in the slums of Calcutta.

Allow me to share some of my favourite quotes from this remarkable woman :

- Not all of us can do only small things with great love.
- Peace begins with a smile.
- If you judge people, you have no time to love them.
- Kind words can be short and easy to speak, but their echoes are truly endless.
- If you can't feed a hundred people, then feed just one.
- Spread love everywhere you go. Let no one ever come to you without leaving happier.
- Be faithful in small things, because it is in them that your strength lies.
- If we have no peace, it is because we have forgotten that we belong to each other.
- Yesterday is gone. Tomorrow has not yet come. We have only today. Let us begin.
- Every time you smile at someone, it is an action of love, a gift to that person, a beautiful thing.

And another quote from Saint Teresa, which resonates with me:

"You will teach them to fly, but they will not fly your flight. You will teach them to dream, but they will not dream your dream. You will teach them to live, but they will not live your life. Nevertheless, in every flight, in every life, in every dream, the print of the way you taught them will remain."

Finally, I would like to quote these words from another inspiring role model, the actress and humanitarian, Audrey Hepburn. I always regarded her as the epitome of elegance, in her appearance and the way she spoke and carried herself.

Audrey Hepburn was once asked to reveal her beauty secrets. She wrote this profound text, which was later read at her funeral.

> "To have attractive lips, speak kind words.
>
> To have a loving look, look for the good side of people.
>
> To look skinny, share your food with the hungry.
>
> To have beautiful hair, let a child cross it with his own fingers once a day.
>
> To have beautiful poise, walk knowing you're never alone, because those who love and loved you accompany you.
>
> People, even more than objects, need to be fixed, spoiled, awakened, wanted and saved: never give up on anyone.
>
> Remember, if you ever need a hand, you'll find them at the end of both your arms.
>
> When you become old, you will discover that you have two hands, one to help yourself, the second to help others.
>
> The beauty of a woman is not in the clothes she wears, in her face or in her way of fixing her hair. The beauty of a woman is seen in her eyes, because that is the door open to her heart, the source of her love.
>
> The beauty of a woman doesn't lie in her makeup, but the true beauty in a woman is reflected in her soul.

It is the tenderness that gives love, the passion that it expresses.

The beauty of a woman grows over the years."

Chapter 11

REACHING FOR THE STARS

In my early years in business, I came across men who feared women with potential. This fear left them unable to nurture or trust these women and put their talent to good use. So I eagerly encourage young women who show great potential to reach for the stars, and tell them not to worry if they only brush the treetops in the process. I always look to establish the minimum standards of work that can be expected from a young woman, and then try to encourage her to achieve the highest standards that I believe she is capable of.

I'm especially keen to see women from migrant backgrounds flourish because, of course, I can relate to their situations, their challenges and opportunities. In recent years, I took on a former Chinese international student whose visa allowed her to remain here, working for two years. Soon after, I also took on a young Indian student. I loved seeing the two young women, Bonita and Garima, working together and encouraging each other.

I see it as a personal challenge to help young women understand and believe in themselves. Some years ago, I became involved with a couple I knew and their 12-year-old daughter. The parents wanted her to move to a new school, but she was adamantly resisting because it would mean leaving her friends. The parents told me of their dilemma, so I took the girl out to dinner. I told her about my experience and how I always saw life changes as opportunities. And that the new school her parents had proposed for her was the one I had set my heart on when I was her age

– but my parents couldn't afford it. My story convinced her to change schools, and she ended up loving her new environment.

***

Many industry insiders wonder how a 'beauty queen' could have achieved so much in her career. I don't think they considered that a beauty queen might also have a brain!

Looking back on nearly 40 years in PR, I can see I did the hard yards to build my profile and my business. It's been a tough road, I've seen a lot of buzzwords come and go, and I've travelled many peaks and troughs, but I have gone the distance – and survived.

Back in 2004, according to my journal, was the first time I contemplated retirement, or at least slowing down. But I went beyond that with my drive and determination, continuing for another 17 years. Even when there are disappointments, you need resilience to succeed in business. Frankly, I'm concerned about the lack of resilience I see in many young men and women today.

I rarely see that essential quality I always valued, the determination to take on a challenge and see it through to the end. Nor do I often see the willingness to stay put and learn as much as you can; to offer loyalty to your employer and relish doing so. I'd love to see more young people consider the obstacles they confront as learning platforms, instead of a reason to quit.

I have never been a quitter. Also, I believe that my instinct to always set the ground rules at the start of any business relationship has been vital to my success. And while I was always ready to put my staff on a pedestal and build them up, I always imparted to them any criticisms clients had of their work.

Over the years, many technological advances have given PR a slick edge and, while we can deliver faster, that has also hardened the way we think and feel. This has somewhat neutered the intimacy that personal contact generates. Many of us read our news online rather than in newspapers or magazines. This and other changes resulting from the digital age have seen freneticism become an obsession. As the Welsh tramp, poet and writer William Henry Davies (1871-1946) wrote: "What is this life if full of care, We have no time to stand and stare?"

There is no downtime for the brain anymore. Does it need to be stimulated all the time? We are in danger of losing contact with ourselves. When I go for my morning walk, I like to hear the songs of the birds and the rustle of the leaves on the trees. I want to hear the slight murmur of traffic at 6.30 am on Beaconsfield Parade. All of that makes it a perfect start to my day. I don't want some cacophonous music coming from an iPhone stuck in my ear.

PR in the Millennial timeframe is in danger of losing its relevance. I achieved what I did through hard work and dedication, not by clock-watching. And there was a time when the client helped you on the journey. That doesn't happen these days. For example, when I had the Whirlpool account, then Managing Director Mike O'Neill worked with me to rebuild the brand in Australia. In PR, you need that vital interaction with the client, that exchange of ideas, because so many little gems can emerge.

There is an old saying that defines success as that which "comes to those who dare to act, and seldom goes to the timid." I am proud of the success I have achieved, so much of which is down to my A-Z of golden rules:

- **A**ttention to detail
- **B**eing attuned to the client's bottom line
- **C**onsistency/**C**ollaboration
- **D**elivery/**D**eadlines/**D**ue diligence
- **E**fficiency

- Fearless with focus
- General knowledge
- Honesty
- Integrity
- Juggling/Judgement
- Keen eye
- Look/Learn/Leap ahead
- Memory
- No/Now/New business
- Observe/Opportunities
- Prepare/Process and Procedure
- Quick to decide/Quick to recall
- Responsiveness
- Smile and Share
- Tenacity
- Ups and Downs
- Verify
- Weigh up
- X-factor
- Yes, we can do it
- Zing (put it into everything you say and do)

I look at this list and know, also, that they are rules that can apply to many other businesses. They can also apply to your personal life or other endeavours. Such as being in the hurly-burly of life as a busy Councillor at the City of Melbourne.

Chapter 12

MARKETING MELBOURNE

It's long hours, hard work, often thankless and barely pays. What would interest anyone in becoming a Councillor in Local Government? Well, for me, it goes back to my childhood and a hardware store.

When my family first came to Australia and we lived in St Kilda, two of my brothers managed to find part-time work at Brock's Hardware on Inkerman Street. And the owner's son-in-law, and Director, John Staughton - a wonderful, kind and respectful man - helped get my brothers their summer jobs and a start to their new lives.

John did so much to help our family – and many others – to settle into new lives in Australia. Especially us Ceylonese because, you have to remember, this was the 1960s; Ceylonese who came to Melbourne moved into Noble Park and Frankston, they did *not* move into St Kilda!

John Staughton was such an inviting presence in all our lives, and he was so encouraging to my brothers. I looked at him and thought, "Geez, you're really special. I want to be like you one day. When I'm older, I want to do the sorts of things for others that you're doing for us."

John Staughton was not only a St Kilda City Councillor, he was also Mayor of St Kilda at the time. Thanks to his example, I'd always had in the back of my mind that I might like to one day be a Councillor myself. In 2011, when I decided the time was right for me to act on that inkling, I was living on St Kilda Road; it made sense, given my locality and John's influence, for me to wander down to St Kilda Town Hall and see if it was something I could do.

But it didn't eventuate; St Kilda Council by then had become the City of Port Phillip and, politically, it was a bit too 'Green' for me. And then I found myself working in the City of Melbourne's precinct. I started talking to Irene Goonan, a friend and former Manningham Mayor, about how I might get onto Melbourne City Council. She suggested I contact Councillor Stephen Mayne, a journalist I'd known since his days at the *Sun News-Pictorial*, and see if I could get on a ticket with him. While I wasn't totally averse to the idea, I did feel I'd prefer to run as an independent.

However, soon after that, I was surprised to receive a call from then Lord Mayor, Robert Doyle.

It is strange that, even coming from where I had in the PR world, working with numerous powerful men like Solomon Lew and Tony D'Aloisio, I still felt intimidated by them. It was the same when I received that call from Robert.

I think my apprehension has something to do with failing my matriculation all those years ago. But, as in the past, I didn't let any sense of inferiority I may have felt stop me from taking the opportunity that Robert's call represented.

It was too good to be true; he wanted to put me on his ticket when elections came up for what would be for him a second term as Lord Mayor. I had met him at functions previously, so I knew him. And, through my long and abiding friendship with then Deputy Lord Mayor Susan Riley, I'd also got to know a little bit about how Robert operated as Mayor.

Susan and I are very close and I've often been there to help guide her from a public relations and reputation perspective. Before I joined council, I was working in Darwin for a few months when I got a call from Susan.

"I've just been elected as Deputy, Beverley," she said. "But Robert's not respecting me as his Deputy. His Chief of Staff is virtually Chief of Staff *and* Deputy."

I told her, "You've got to deal with that situation straightaway. Give him clear direction about what you want." I even wrote down for her the way I thought she should handle the situation. Within weeks Susan rang back saying she'd had success; Robert had admitted he needed to do more in acknowledging her as his Deputy, and that's what happened.

What I didn't realise then – and failed to remember when I began to get involved in running for Council that first time – was that this was *politics*. I had no idea and, looking back, I can't believe that I didn't realise it. But, in some ways, I *do* understand my thinking; I wanted to be on Council to serve, and the politics side of it was something that held little interest for me. Yet, as a Councillor, you simply can't avoid the politics.

When Robert interviewed me to be on his ticket in 2012, he and his team had me well-researched. After a wide-ranging interview, he said he'd love to have me on the team. Along with Susan Riley as Deputy Mayor, the other members of the team would be Arron Wood, Kevin Louey and me.

I said, okay, I'll join. He was happy, but said I'd need to invest some money. Coming from a public relations background, that to me was logical. He said he needed $30,000 so that's what I donated to the campaign.

I didn't hear much for months and then it all suddenly got cracking, with photoshoots and a campaign launch. In October 2012, I was officially a City of Melbourne Councillor and engaged in the full political show. But the great thing about Robert was that he never, ever shoved politics at us. He never said you've got to vote this way because it is what the Liberals would prefer. He always showed us his reasoning and demonstrated his thinking. He still wanted us to vote as a team – although I didn't on a couple of occasions. He wasn't happy, but he never took me to task about it.

So, to an extent, I had freedom of conscience, but Robert framed the voting around what was necessary for loyalty to the team. And when you hear words like that . . . of course you'd want to be seen as loyal, wouldn't you? I did have a bit of fear around voting in a way that Robert wouldn't like because, inherently, I don't like doing anything wrong! I can't do anything wrong by anyone knowingly and then say I didn't know!

Initially, the Council setting, having to vote and be part of a team – not being the boss – was a huge change for me. I found myself becoming very quiet, on Council and everywhere. I became almost withdrawn. And I depended a lot on Councillor Stephen Mayne, with whom I shared an office, to help me understand my new role.

It wasn't long, however, before I loved being on Council.

Because of my PR background, I was made chair of the Marketing Melbourne portfolio. It was an exciting portfolio, that also took in retail, hospitality and small business. And I got cracking trying to make little changes that I hoped would have big results.

When I started on Council, the Melbourne Spring Fashion Week (now Melbourne Fashion Week) was limited to RMIT Fashion Design students. I fiercely advocated for change so that all five of Melbourne's institutions offering fashion design could be involved – namely RMIT, Holmesglen, Kangan Batman, Whitehouse and Box Hill. It took two years, but I got that change through! For me, that was a big achievement because it went to the heart of giving people the opportunities they need. The fashion show raises our fashion standards, and I wanted a level playing field for all fashion students. Now, the involvement of all those institutions works brilliantly with links even to a Japanese fashion school.

I was also really proud to get a city-based Men's Shed up and running – even though it wasn't part of my portfolio. Frankly, it was something I was going to do even if I hadn't got onto Council. My late journalist friend, Glenda Banks, a really formidable woman, had called me in May 2012 before the Council election and said, "Bev, can you come and talk to my mates in East Melbourne, there's a predicament about their men."

I had no idea then that when you get on Council you could take up these causes, put them as your little red dot on the annual plan. And Lord Mayor Doyle helped me greatly there; he guided it, lobbied State Government and helped make it happen at Fed Square, which was very special. To this day, I maintain my connection with the executive, including the president, Andrew Stefanetti.

It was a very simple achievement, but it was important to me because my good friend, David Bardas, lost his business and found himself suddenly alone at home with nothing to do. David's wife was frustrated with him being at home – after not being there for 40 years! He ended up writing a play called *Home for Lunch*, and I did the PR for it. So many men of a certain age are retired at home with nothing to do and his story resonated with me because men don't often talk to each other about what's going on inside. This recently was reaffirmed by Dr Michael Carr-Gregg who in an interview with Neil Mitchell talked about young girls and how they share their stories, make eye contact with each other while building relationships in the school yard. Boys, however, will engage in a punch-up and a race to win, with little or no conversation and limited, if any, eye contact.

So often, men at home with nothing to do meant women going bananas because of it. Either way, it was a mental health issue that needed solving. I know that Men's Sheds help. I heard a comment recently that Men's Sheds are just clubs. But, even leaving aside all of the interaction they have with students and the work they do for charities, I think they help men and we need more of them. And we certainly don't need Women's Sheds. Women are already much better at talking to each other and getting things happening between them. Anyway, membership of the Melbourne Men's Shed program is open to women, if they desire. In fact I recently became a member myself!

As well as the Melbourne Men's Shed, I was also pleased to have been involved in getting the 2014 AIDS Conference off the ground. I wasn't a big part of it, but my experience as a committee member, working with Fran Kerlin (formerly Morris) was amazing. Fran had been one of my first clients in PR and later worked at the City of Melbourne. And she and I just *got* each other! We realised that partners of delegates attending the conference would be looking for things to do. (Around 14,000 delegates attended, and some 6,000 were joined by partners). We created opportunities, like shopping and wine tours for them, which offered great economic spin-offs for Melbourne, the state and small businesses.

Another wonderful opportunity that I really enjoyed was the chance to tour China and Japan with Lord Mayor Doyle and several Councillors in 2014. I was amazed at the reverence with which Chinese and Japanese people treated Robert. It was like he was a king. And his performances at meetings, signings of memoranda and in understanding other cultures was outstanding. You're speaking through an interpreter, but you've got to keep your eyes peeled to read body language and other signs. Robert was a master at it.

Being on Council, while also still running my business, was like a tornado that instead of blowing out, just keeps going and going. It was like having two full-time jobs – but Council only paid a part-time wage. It left me with virtually no time to continue the charity work that I had so much enjoyed with figures like Father Bob. Then, in 2016, my mother fell seriously ill for the third time. I found myself having to regularly care for her while at the same time living with a stepson with autism and his twin preparing to come out.

I haven't mentioned yet that I married Russell Mortimer in January 2012. He had the care of two teenage sons, twins, from his previous marriage. So our union was a major adjustment for him and the boys, as well as for me.

Then, barely four months into our marriage, I was canvassing with him the idea of running for Council on Robert Doyle's ticket.

We had several discussions and weighed up the pros and cons, including my lifelong ambition to extend my commitment to community by incorporating civic contribution. Russell recognised that this was important for me, a chance to realise an ambition that was inspired by my deep appreciation of John Staughton in his days as St Kilda's Mayor (1968-69).

Perhaps I charted a course way back then; a path that would see me excel in the People City Portfolio in my second term at the City of Melbourne. A course that shows how children can be influenced and how ambition can be instilled and fostered for decades ahead. As well, a route to compassion, care and connectedness with the very cohort that I worked for as Chair of the People City Portfolio.

While I yearned for mum to live to beyond the age of 90, I knew that she was weakening and her health was worsening. It was at this time that I started strengthening myself to face life without my mum. Her tenacity, strong will, faith and loyalty to family kept her going for 37 years beyond the death of my father.

I knew that something had to give, and it was fortuitous that I did not get elected in the 2016 elections. Looking back, I hadn't given my campaign for re-election 100%. I wasn't disappointed to be forced to step away from being a City of Melbourne Councillor.

I'd already almost lost mum on two occasions before I left Council in October 2016. I'd even begun collecting photographs for video memorials and talking to my graphic designer about making a funeral booklet. I'd cried and grieved while taking on the responsibility of making sure her sisters saw her before she passed. Mum survived those two scares, but in 2016 I knew things were different.

When I left Council, it felt very much like God was guiding me, telling me it had all been too much, and now was the time to focus on mum. I accepted it and it was a relief. And mum was delighted that I would be there to help her, even more.

Despite her protestations earlier that year, I had to move her into a nursing home. She was an amazing cook, but when she was regularly burning her own Sri Lankan dishes, I thought, "It's time". She was excited at first, then she refused and wouldn't hear of the idea. I told her she wasn't coping anymore and she had to do it, but she wouldn't. So I said, "Okay, I'm going and you'll never see me again." A couple of days later she called and said, "Okay, I'll go." It wasn't like it was alien to her. Her sister had been placed in the same nursing home six months prior.

With the help of my brother, Sandy, I finalized her placement in Arcare Nursing Home, in Keysborough. I'd always visited her weekly, but I would ring her every other day. Now, without any Council work to occupy my time, I was able to visit her at least three times a week. During this period, I kept running my business with just one client (a very important one - Russell's business, QA Software), and didn't crank it up so soon after Council elections. I just wanted to be there for mum.

My grieving process that had begun after her first illnesses continued throughout her final months. And it was a complex grieving process because we hadn't always seen eye to eye. I'd always had no doubt she loved me, but she'd never demonstrated that love for me. Until two weeks before she passed.

I'd brought my brother Sandy down from Darwin because she seemed very close to death at the time. And she looked at him, then me, and said, "What would we all have done without Beverley?" That was the strongest and most definitive acknowledgement I ever got of mum's love for me, and her gratitude for the support she could always rely on.

It felt to me that was the sealer, her time was coming. After Sandy went back to Darwin two or three days later, I said to mum, "You've seen Sandy, you can now let go." Which I knew she was going to.

When mum passed in September 2017, I intended to crank up my business again. But before that, I went away with my third brother, Durand for a holiday in South Australia's Barossa Valley. And that's when all hell broke loose at the City of Melbourne.

Chapter 13

TROUBLE AT COUNCIL

Holidaying in the Barossa, I wasn't watching television or connecting to the internet. I was having a complete break from the media and the endless streams of information that were part of my working life. But suddenly on a Saturday I was receiving all these text messages from people asking whether I was "coming back" and what was I going to do. I wasn't in a mood to respond to them, I was having reflective time with my brother, but I did wonder, "What are they all talking about?"

Then, on the Sunday after the scandal involving the Lord Mayor hit the news, I got a call from a friend in Thailand. Anthony asked the same questions that had been in the text messages and I asked what the hell was he talking about? He said, "You better watch the news."

I caught up with the news on my phone, and the next morning I received phone calls from every radio station, all asking if I would come back to Council. But I didn't know anything, really, about what had gone on at Council, or the details of what had happened with Robert or what might happen next. I really didn't know what I would do, and I was still feeling very raw after mum's passing. If I was thinking anything about my life, it was that I would focus on my business and work in the Chinese market helping foreign companies wanting to break into Australia.

But suddenly, I had this big decision to make about whether I should come back to Council.

***

For those who don't remember, 'Hell broke loose' at the City of Melbourne when the media reported that two female Councillors had complained that they had been sexually harassed by the Lord Mayor. Robert Doyle denied the allegations, saying that his actions and comments had been misinterpreted. But he resigned as Lord Mayor, and as a Councillor, in February 2018.

An independent investigation by Melbourne City Council found that the two Councillors had been 'sexually harassed' by the Lord Mayor, and their workplace was unsafe. Victoria Police also investigated whether any sexual crimes had been committed, and announced in June 2020 that no charges would be laid.

All of this happened when I wasn't a Councillor. But I sincerely believe that if I had been a Councillor at the time, the outcome may have been different. I would have said things and done things that could have changed the outcome.

I'm one who always opts for saying, 'I need to talk to you, let's sit down and talk this through'. I don't know the sequence of events, but it appears to me that Robert was treated harshly when he first learned about the serious career-destroying allegations against him in the media. Then on the Sunday, City of Melbourne CEO, Ben Rimmer, called Robert to a meeting that day in the CBD, where Robert was informed that Dr Ian Freckleton, QC, had been commissioned to investigate the allegations made against him.

If I was in Ben Rimmer's shoes at the time, I'd have called an emergency meeting of Councillors. I might have consulted Robert's staff, particularly those women who worked for him. Let me just say that I think Robert deserved more assistance than he received. Suddenly, investigations were being launched and everything moved far too rapidly.

***

I wasn't comfortable at the time with the '#MeToo' conversation, and I'm still not. I think as a society we are putting too much effort into blowing the gender trumpet. And one of the initiatives I dislike immensely is the Male Champions of Change. I don't need a man to effect change or herald it for me. I find it inherently regressive. I wonder if some of those who pressured Robert to stand down did so to enhance their credentials as Male Champions of Change.

Robert Doyle was a 'touchy-feely' sort of person. I don't see anything wrong with that. A lot of men and women from my generation are like that, it's a personality trait. I believe there are two individuals in a situation, and not all men are abusers. So I find it very difficult to agree with this '#MeToo' frame of mind. If abuse has occurred, it absolutely cannot and should not be tolerated. But I just don't think you can slam men who are naturally tactile. I know I can be like that myself.

Some years ago, I was at a funeral and I had a strong emotional flashback. At the time, I was sitting next to a male Councillor and instinctively put my hand on his thigh to steady myself, as a comfort. He asked, "Are you okay?" and I told him what had happened. So, does that mean that at some stage he could say that I touched him up? With the current thinking, it seems so. I think that's really sad.

There is a lot of talk now about keeping physicality out of the workplace altogether. (Remember the pre-COVID 19 era, when people would shake hands?) I couldn't handle a no-physical-contact regime. I've always touched people, and I come from a culture where we touch, we're very expressive with our hands, similar to Italians. It would alter the way I feel and operate. It would almost turn me into a zombie. No thank you!

My point is that not every physical contact between a man and a woman should be assumed to have a sexual intention. Another point I would make from Robert Doyle's demise as Lord Mayor is this: women can't be seeking out power and stature and the strengthening of their role, but then seize the first opportunity to throw the '#MeToo' card at those men who are best placed to help them get that power, or help them understand its use. I think there needs to be a lot more flexibility and understanding. And I am saying that as someone who had her own encounter with Robert Doyle, when I was on Council the first time.

As I've said, Robert was by nature a 'touchy feely' person. He could be tough on me as a Councillor, but socially was always very friendly. He'd always plant a kiss on my cheek, which is what I do to people, too. However, I never went out of my way to socialise within his circle; I had enough circles of my own. So I didn't provoke any behaviour from him beyond a friendly hug and a kiss on the cheek.

On Tuesday nights, all the Councillors socialised together. One Tuesday, he was inebriated, he'd had quite a bit to drink that afternoon. In fact, there was a lot of drinking going on amongst the male Councillors. I was undergoing a very traumatic time in my life, it being the first of the three times I'd begun to feel mum's health was failing badly and I would soon lose her. It really rocked me. And I wasn't getting on with my husband Russell very well; I was having difficulties with both boys living with us and, as I've mentioned, one of them lives with autism.

Unbeknown to me, Susan Riley had told Robert of the family issues I was having. So, he led me out of the dining room into his office, literally by hand, and said "Come with me, talk to me". All the Councillors noticed it and, I admit, I was worried.

In his office, I opened up to him about everything that was going on in my life. And he offered me genuine concern. I had a glass of Rosé with him and when I got up to leave, he kissed me goodbye as I turned my cheek to him. He wasn't forceful. It was almost, to me, the sort of kiss that your grandma would give you. It was fondness, saying I care about you, the pressures in here at Council, and the pressures you're feeling on all fronts outside of here. So I didn't take offence or nurse any grievance about it.

***

Across 25 years of being in state and local government, Robert Doyle has left an indelible mark. He put Melbourne very much on the map and forged tremendous relationships with politicians and the bureaucracy in China and Japan. His genuine love and passion for Melbourne could never be doubted.

It's hard yakka being a Councillor, and even more so being Lord Mayor. His contribution to Melbourne was huge and I think that people should be grateful to Robert for having done so much for the city.

I still stay in contact with Robert and we catch up occasionally. In the same year that the situation occurred with Robert, I had to cope with the deaths of five close friends. What happened with Robert was the icing on a pretty sour cake. Some days, I almost wanted to put a doona over my head and say, "No, I'm not here and I don't want to be part of this conversation".

I was incensed when I saw an article in the *Herald-Sun*, linking my name to a gossip item about Councillors pressuring Robert to resign. This wasn't true, and I contacted the editor to make it clear that I wanted the story to be corrected. He quickly did so.

***

At first, when people suggested I return to Council after Robert left, I was certain I didn't want to. It was even suggested I run for Lord Mayor. But I had deference towards Councillor Arron Wood and didn't want to upset anything he was planning, whether that was a tilt at Mayor or Deputy. And I'd given Sally Capp my word previously that I wouldn't run. That was also important to me – it always is – to stick by my word.

Still, it was a tumultuous few weeks in late 2017 as I considered whether or not I would stand for Council election. And I remained for a long time on the side of not re-joining; I still, after all, had my mother's last words in my ears: "Look after Russell." But, as the coverage of Robert Doyle and the allegations against him became deeper, I began to think that the Councillors who would still be around from the last term would appreciate a familiar face, and the new ones could do with a steady hand.

I returned to Council in January 2018 and I served as chair of the People City portfolio. It was the portfolio I wanted and it suited me perfectly. It gave me energy because I am interested in all people, from the streets to high places, and I enjoy being a 'connector'.

I encountered a strange thing when I started on Council again: people, both inside and outside Council, kept asking, "Is 'team Doyle' going to continue?" What a ridiculous question! My response was, "Hang on! *What* 'team Doyle'?"

When I was sworn in again as a Councillor, I asked Father Bob Maguire to attend, and to bless the Council chambers. I believed that a toxic atmosphere had developed in that workplace, and a cleansing ceremony could only help.

I soon swung back into my normal rhythm as a Councillor, with the addition of helping first-time Councillors navigate their journeys. And Deputy Lord Mayor Arron Wood, who was acting in the Lord Mayor's role, said it was good to have me back because I thought about things. I believe that is a strength I brought to Council; I went away and thought things through quietly and came back with something perhaps others hadn't thought about – because they were too busy doing the political thing. For me, being on Council involved no personal or material gain. I was just doing some good work, doing my best to bring good people together.

***

It was difficult to straddle my entrepreneurial side with the political side of me that being on Council represented. And I felt I'd often gone outside the zone when it came to what was expected of Councillors.

A case in point for me was working with community groups – like Travellers Aid, Joy FM and a few others who in my final term were going to be evicted from their City Village premises, due to major building renovations. They had to find new premises, that's just how it was, and, as a Councillor, that's where my involvement could stop. But I began to put the word out there for those organisations to help them find new space and I did all I could to help them. It was one of the difficulties of being on Council, not knowing quite where my role started and stopped!

I loved working on Council, loved working with Deputy Lord Mayor Wood and with Councillor Jackie Watts, my deputy in the People City portfolio. Jackie and I didn't start off well: she sent me a text message meant for someone else, claiming I only came back to Council for the publicity and the money. I was genuinely upset to think she would believe this. But we had to work together, and I came to appreciate her insights, contributions and intelligence.

The truth is, that I donated more than $16,000, the first six months of my annual stipend to Father Bob! I did this because I knew of the pressures that the Father Bob Maguire Foundation was under, in trying to provide scholarships to children whose future prospects would be improved if their school fees could be paid.

You wouldn't be a Councillor for the money if you didn't have to – and I didn't have to. It was just work I'd committed myself to doing. So, if I hadn't been paid, I would still have done it.

I love to take people out to lunch, and while on Council I connected with stakeholders over lunch and I did that on my money. Not boozy lunches; I just like the exchange you can have when you're breaking bread. It might be something to do with my Catholic religion, but breaking bread to me is a spiritual thing that draws people closer to each other and creates lots of new ideas and thinking.

After the 2020 election, I knew it was my last stint on Council. I won't consider running again. I did the main thing I wanted to do in my last term in the People City portfolio, trying to do more to change the situation for those experiencing homelessness, as well as being a strong and committed advocate for the disabled.

I was delighted to learn last year that the United Nations and the World Health Organisation had declared 3 December 2022 the first annual International Day of Persons with Disabilities. This is designed to raise awareness on behalf of the world's 1.3million disabled people of the challenges they face, and to secure their rights to participate fully and equally in society. Our fellow citizens who live with disabilities need the support and the confidence of all of us to be able to achieve their dreams. To dream is not only within the ambit of those who are physically and mentally able.

***

It wasn't until I started in the People City portfolio – and I began doing some work in the area of homelessness – that I remembered my family's experience of couch-surfing. Council was talking a lot about keeping the emphasis on people sleeping rough on the streets, not couch surfers because, of course, it's Council's responsibility to manage what's happening on the city's streets. But I felt a pang and wanted there to be emphasis on couch-surfing because that is homelessness, too. I'm sure some people were thinking 'what is she on about?', but something had triggered in me – and then I realised it was what my family and I had experienced.

I brought my heart to the work with homeless people. It was from a position of not needing to do it to get something in return. Mine wasn't a political decision to help this cohort, I did it because I empathised with them, having gone through my own experience of couch-surfing and having nowhere to go. And that was at the age of six.

It was part of that ability to look to the needs of the other person that I managed to develop when I was younger. I have also suppressed a hell of a lot, but we need to keep going and not always sit back and wonder what is in it for me. *Quid quo pro*, which I learnt from Alan Chipp, isn't always the way. And I've known that since I was a kid. Friends from Ceylon recently reminded me how I shared my lunch with other kids, that I was a very assured young leader who cared for everyone else, from sharing my food to helping others with homework, to always looking out for them. I was trying to create a world where if I looked after the next person, they would look after me if the need should arise. This was at a time when I was experiencing poverty and family violence, but no matter how broken-spirited you are, if you look after the next person, there is a gift in it that you get back. One of my friends said, "Didn't you just hate it that they took your food?" and I said they didn't *take* my food, I *shared* it! I shared whatever meagre meal I had because I wanted other kids to taste my mother's cooking – and to give them an experience of me. Because perhaps they were not much better off than I was. I thought I was the poorest kid in school, but maybe I wasn't.

So, those acts as a girl seem to have got me thinking and kept me thinking the way I do: there is always going to be someone who needs a helping hand, and it may not be always obvious who that is.

***

One of the first things I got involved with when it came to Council's work with homelessness was to make sure Victoria Police were better integrated around the discussion table.

Previously, VicPol hadn't even been invited to be on the City of Melbourne discussion table regarding homelessness. I said, "Guys, I want you in the camp". Police are at the grassroots when it comes to homelessness, they even have a Senior Sergeant in charge of it. That is perfect for us at the City of Melbourne, I thought, imagine what we could learn from them?

So we made a place for them, but then there was concern they would come in uniform and that would upset the people with lived experience who were at the discussion table. I called Inspector Craig Peel and said, "Would you be okay to wear civvies to this meeting?" and he happily agreed. So we began to benefit from their input. The City of Melbourne's compliance team does a wonderful job, and, along with them, police are not sidelined when it comes to homelessness and the City's genuine efforts to make change.

We need more transitional accommodation. It doesn't have to be housing for every person, but we need to be providing better forms of accommodation. We have the money to do it, but we don't have the land. And that's a big conundrum because the land has to be in the City of Melbourne's boundaries.

So homelessness was my big focus during my last stint at Council and I applied the philosophy that I think is vital when it comes to how we do social welfare: the old saying about a man plucked out of a boat at sea and the rescuer saying to the victim, "Give me your hand!" But upon changing that to, "No, take my hand," the man does just that and is saved. I have always remembered that. Perhaps I have too often allowed people to take my hand, but my hand is always there!

It was the same in the area of disability; I was constantly at my fellow Councillors to do more for the people with disability living in our city, and I know as I write this that my efforts were seen and heard out there. The overarching thing I feel I've done is give the sector a voice in council.

I used my own personal situation, being step-parent to Andre, who lives with autism, and that has helped me to understand the issues that people with disability face, and it has amplified my voice for those who are cognitively impaired. I have been able to give *them* a voice at Town Hall, because previously it was mostly about physical disability.

I gave each member of the disability advisory committee a seamless touch point into Town Hall and its processes. There were several people with disability on the committee and they always knew I was there, urging and pushing for them. I fought very hard about the issue of motorcycles on our footpaths, bringing home the fact that they are an impediment to people with disability; they have trouble getting out of their cars or getting their equipment out of their cars. There have been terrible stories of people with disability waiting for hours in the heat to get back in their cars because a motorcycle was blocking their car door. So, my work resulted in signs being put up regarding how motorcyclists can park on our footpaths.

All of that led the Victorian Government to listen and care more about our congested footpaths in Melbourne. I really worry about access for people with canes, assistance dogs, people with wheelchairs – and the elderly. I put the elderly into the disability sector because we are an ageing population and this city in future will have many more elderly people with mobility issues, whether they are visitors or city residents. As I think to what I want to see happen next, my first thought is that we need to decongest tramstops for people with disability and elderly people. I also think we need to ban e-scooters from footpaths.

***

I know I tried to cram a lot into being a Councillor. I remember once I met 35 new people in one day! That's very hard to deal with, trying to remember names and trying to engage with all those people in a meaningful way. But that is in many ways the task and responsibility all Councillors have in front of them. Yet it works both ways; you gain a lot from meeting that many people, experiencing their stories and realities.

I learnt a hell of a lot from being a City of Melbourne Councillor. It amplified my ability to connect people with each other, and I feel I helped a lot of people and helped the city. I'm at a point now where I can take great satisfaction from seeing these things flourish from the outside, rather than being on Council.

I think I will always be part of the landscape of Melbourne, in some shape or form, giving back to a community I love so much. Because that's what I saw Council work as: *putting back*. It was my service to the community. And there is a big role for all of us in that, we need to herald it to everyone: at some stage in your life you need to think about how you can serve. But the problem is, when it comes to local government, it gets caught up with political sludge. I say I wasn't a politician, but former Governor General Quentin Bryce picked me up on that. She said, "Everyone's a politician, Beverley". While I know there is truth in that, I prefer, then, to think that I was a diplomat rather than a politician.

And a diplomat is, of course, what we often need to be in our home lives.

Chapter 14

THIRD TIME LUCKY

By 2009, I'd been married twice, but on my own for 12 years. It was before my time on council, so I was even thinking of retiring down at Portsea. I was feeling very comfortable about being on my own. That independence is something I got from my mother who, after my father died aged 53, was very stoic.

So, retirement or not, I was at that time definitely wanting to start *feeling* life the way I wanted to.

I had a very strict work regime. I was – and still am – very structured in what I do. I used to do my prep work for the office the night before and, when my alarm went off, I'd get up, go for a walk and grab breakfast on the run. I've always worked a few doors or tram stops away from where I've lived, so that has helped make my routine efficient.

But back in 2009, that was about to change significantly after a chance meeting at a reunion dinner for my brothers' school.

Every year, St Peter's College, Colombo, holds a reunion dinner dance in Melbourne, a way of bringing together former students from Sri Lanka. My brothers, of course, all went to St Peter's, and I encouraged them to attend the dances, sometimes going along myself. In May 2009, I'd just returned from doing some work in Darwin and I wasn't that interested in going to the event at Malvern Town Hall, but three girlfriends from Ceylon said, "You've got to come, you really do." Unbeknown to me, my friends were trying to match-make me with a man they knew.

I don't remember engaging too much with the man they had in mind, but I do remember meeting Russell Mortimer, someone my brothers knew from their early school days in Ceylon. I had vague memories of him as a six-year-old, so when he talked to me at the event it wasn't a complete surprise. He asked me how I was going and said that he knew about some of the frustrations I had with my older brother. Russell told me he'd lost his sister in the past year and encouraged me to do whatever I could to mend the relationship.

I said I loved my brother very much, Russell gave me his card if I needed to contact him, and that was about the end of the conversation. Then, in August that year, I got a call from Russell saying he'd like to have lunch and talk about PR for his software business. I said, "Terrific, let's do that." We talked PR, but then he began to tell me about his marriage not being so good.

I started to get a bit nervous and said, "I can fix your company's PR profile, but I can't fix your marriage." Still, I agreed to work on his PR and got cracking straight away. In December, at our monthly client meeting, he told me about a cruise he was planning to take with his family. I said, "Hey, here's a chance to reconnect with your wife. Standing on the deck and looking towards the horizon, that would be a nice time for you to try to reconnect and build some bridges."

Two weeks after the cruise, he rang me and said he'd like to see me. I said okay and, when we met, he said he was planning to leave his wife and was I single? I said, "Hang on a minute, if you want to leave, you leave. And, actually, I am seeing someone right now, it's not going anywhere, but that is beside the point."

Four weeks later, he left his wife, and our relationship started soon after. We've now been together for 13 years, married for eleven. My relationship with Russell is the longest and most stable I've had in my life.

Despite growing up there, I'd never been out with a Sri Lankan-born man. Culturally, I was always somewhere else: Europe, and especially Italy. And I love Australia, of course. So being with Russell was something very new – and I don't cook Sri Lankan curries! I cook a mean Thai curry, but I'd never had to cook a Sri Lankan curry because if I wanted my fix of that I just went to my mother's house. But I think with my cooking I won over Russell and his boys, Andre and Jake, pretty quickly!

Something that I liked about Russell from the outset was that he was very close to his family, and very family-orientated. Families are complex; and I've got one of the more complex families, and yet he understood my family situation instinctively. He'd had insight into my family through my brothers, but he hadn't, of course, seen my side. Once he saw who I am – who I've become and the importance I place on family – that sunk in very deep for him. Family can do no wrong for me, which is a tough position to be in because I tend to become the whipping girl. But I am always there for my family because it's what God gave us and, in terms of building our character, it's a case of iron sharpening iron. I brought that family orientation and selflessness into my relationship with Russell and his children because it permeates everything I do; I am constantly thinking about how to help others because my life is wrapped up in people.

I was also attracted to the fact that Russell had worked to establish a successful business. He had put in the hard yards, and that is something I really value. I have great admiration and respect for anyone who starts a business from the ground up, with no family money, and something that is their own idea or innovation, not someone else's bright idea. I admire the hard slog, the time it takes to finish your education first – and then to work for someone else, knowing that all the while you're going to do something for yourself and employ people.

Russell, an engineer turned IT expert, started his business, QA Software Pty Ltd, in his Melbourne loungeroom. But he went back to Sri Lanka in the mid-90s to set up the back office he needed. One day in 1998, in walked an 18-year-old with a CV in his pocket, ready to give Russell his thoughts about IT. The young man had broad stature and eyes that were deep, deep brown – and gleaming with excitement to meet someone like Russell, who was likewise excited about IT's possibilities.

Russell could tell this young man had the smarts. They had a conversation and Russell said, "You've got the job." The young man said, "I've brought you my CV to look at," but Russell said, "I don't need to look at that. You've convinced me you're the one I need."

That guy, Sivaram, stayed with Russell for the entire 25 years of his business. A young man of Tamil origin, who would have gone through hell in the deepest times of conflict in Sri Lanka. For Russell to bestow upon someone that level of respect and admiration – and inspiration – was brilliant. And that is the richness of being in business – when you can impart things like that without even knowing, just by giving someone a go. To this day, that relationship endures, with tremendous mutual respect.

Starting a business and giving others a go is something that Russell and I are very passionate about. My business was never as big as his, but it was very successful. His was four times as large as mine, but that journey we both travelled at different times, not knowing each other, was about constantly giving someone a go. And I think, for Russell, that's the greatest gift he's given himself – and the 160 staff he had when he sold his business. The fabulous Steven Joustra was his partner in the business, and together they knew when the time had come to sell. It was their baby, really, but they were quick off the mark. When the right suitor came along, they didn't hesitate.

Russell and Steven remain business partners managing a legacy software solution, QDMS, that was not part of the acquisition deal.

Looking at both our businesses, if anyone has the inkling of any idea that could work, then I say try it, do it. Seek the help you need, go out and do it, and attach to others who want to see you succeed. I've carried that throughout my life, and I continue to find people into whom I can have input and so does Russell.

***

Meeting Russell's twin boys, then 16, for the first time was a huge challenge. I immediately got on like a house on fire with Andre, who has autism, but his brother Jake, I could see, was going to be a harder nut to crack.

The important thing I kept in mind at the outset was not to overdo it. I did what came naturally to me and started with good food. Steak and vegetables, always a winner! And I worked on showing them I was helping build a family unit, without taking away from their mother's contribution.

The routine I'd been used to for 12 years, while single, was, however, thrown into chaos! Russell rented a property in Blackburn, the boys' mother lived in Balwyn, and I had my apartment in St Kilda Road. So Fridays was all about ferrying food and clothes to Blackburn, and then ensuring from Friday night on there was a good meal on the table and I was tending to the family's needs. Then I'd come back home to my apartment on a Sunday night and do my chores, filling my fridge for the week and cleaning up. It was very, very tiring, with a lot of driving, but I managed.

Soon after Russell and I got together, my brother, Sandy, visited Russell's ex-wife on one of his trips to Melbourne from Darwin. A staunch Catholic, he went to see her to console her and say that he wasn't in favour of our union. He predicted that it wouldn't last, that Russell would be back with her in six months.

Of course, I was disappointed when I learned of this sometime later. But rather than rebuking him, and potentially risking our relationship, I took a step back to consider his point of view. I realised his intention was not to betray me, but to express how important his religion was to him. I decided that I could respect that. Even if I disagreed, I could respect the strength of his religious convictions.

***

When Russell and I moved in together, Jake lived with us pretty much from day one, which was great. And then we would have Andre with us every second weekend and every second week.

It was a huge learning curve to suddenly have stepsons, one living with autism and the other coming out as gay when he turned 18. But this is where my own charitable nature from the age of 13 came into play – and still does. I always learnt to look out for the other person rather than myself. So that has held me in good stead in caring for Andre's needs, and for Jake's various requests when he was coming out.

I got as much information as I could from friends who had experienced gay friends coming out, and so I listened to Jake and was very mindful of his needs. The whole process happened in a very peaceful and accommodating way, which is how it should be. If there is one word that sums up the coming out process it is that we need to provide young people with *support*, then watch them grow up and everyone reaps the benefits.

I helped see Jake through Year 11 and 12 and helped him find internships and work experience. At one stage he wanted to be a vet, so I helped him be a zookeeper for a day, thinking outside the square and trying to give him opportunities that would set the scene for him when he went to university.

One of the best things Russell and I were able to offer the boys was when we thought it would be fantastic to give Andre a really tremendous overseas experience. But we decided it wouldn't be the same if we took him, so what about if Jake and his partner Tom took him? Jake and Tom agreed, and it was a great time for Andre, hanging out with his brother, and Tom being like another brother, too.

Three weeks was a long time for Jake to have to look after Andre so, before they all left, I said to Tom, "Look after Jake because we don't want him getting stressed." And Tom said, "Don't worry, it will be top of my list."

Jake and Tom have since married, and it was a very joyous occasion.

Through the National Disability Insurance Scheme, Andre has since August 2019 lived in a home in Ashwood with four others. We see him once a fortnight or more, and following a period of regression, which broke my heart, he has now begun to blossom. Living away from home is the best thing for him, even though it has been stressful for Russell, me and Andre's mother. We have all put a lot of time and effort into him, but we have come to terms with the fact that employment is a long-shot, and we are all going to have to be there for his needs. We also know that Jake needs to be set up in life so that he can look after his brother once we all pass away. He will have a big job on his hands for which he assures me he is prepared.

Andre still spends a lot of time with us, mainly on long weekends and 'school holidays', which suits the others in his household. Andre's involvement in Jake and Tom's wedding in Iceland was very special and seamless. Andre dictated his speech to me as I typed it for him, and he delivered it beautifully.

Early in 2018, Russell sold most of his business and now manages one worldwide software product while also running our property portfolio. Jake wanted to join the family business, so he is now up and running with the property arm, learning about property management, construction, project management and developing a range of other skills. It was a huge load off Russell's shoulders to have someone who he can trust and bring through the ranks.

While that experience was valuable for Jake's personal and professional growth, he decided in 2020 that he wanted to pursue a career in education, and he commenced his two-year journey at RMIT.

I think the extended lockdown experience in Victoria (2020-'21) changed our perspectives, for many of us, leading to new and diverse thoughts about how we manage our lives and our personal growth. I think Jake's change of career path is a good example of that. He will go on to be a great teacher.

Chapter 15

WORKING WITH GEN 'WHY?'

In my long career in public relations, I have been seen sometimes as too demanding, someone whose work ethic was too strict, and who had staff too scared to make a mistake. I'm not sure if that's all true, but I have been meticulous in my ways and have never settled for second-best, even when it has involved a small client. My clients expected the best from me every time, and I always respected that in my dealings with them. I treated their business and products as my own and never short-changed them.

I loathe mediocrity. That's why I've always insisted on the best from my staff, at all times. And the truth is I wasn't taught how to be a manager; I started a small business and never realised I also had to be its *manager*. But I worked night and day, moved heaven and earth, and harnessed all my networks, contacts and knowledge for my clients. I never stopped until I was able to get that edge for them. Still, I realise that my attitude is not widely held by younger generations.

The Gen Y phenomenon kept surfacing all the time in my work. To motivate those who are products of Gen Y (or 'Generation Why Me?') is not easy; many of them seem to believe in the misguided philosophy that 'near enough is good enough'. I am not happy with that; the gap between a service and how it is delivered is a wide one.

As my business matured, I kept employing staff who were very much of the Gen Y mould, who thought they were like no other in the world. They showed little respect and had very little loyalty and their 'why not me?', 'why not now?' attitude was often problematic. It doesn't meld with my values and levels of generosity as a charity worker, family member, or simply as a person. Of course, not all of them had that attitude, but enough for me to see it as a disturbing trend.

Too many of the Gen Y people I have encountered are cocky and self-centred. They have to be stimulated all the time and are easily distracted. Some, in an office environment, checked their personal email and sent personal SMSs as soon as they reported for work.

In a typical day, I observed staff spending 15 minutes looking at and responding to personal emails, then their minds wandered for another 15 minutes. That's 30 minutes of quality time they should have devoted to the work I was paying them for! Anything they were thinking before that, which could have been client-related, would be long gone.

My view has always been, "I am here while others are there, and what is it I can do to enhance their position?" You couldn't expect that from many in Gen Y. They only see replicas of themselves. Theirs is a rebellion without a cause – not so much the people, but the generation to which they are attached.

It was so different when I began in the workforce. During my time as a clerk at the Immigration Department, I had a boss who had emigrated from Latvia. Whenever he briefed me on a job he wanted done, I took in every word slowly, sometimes making notes, then I digested them. My goal was to achieve what he wanted – and that little bit more. I was never distracted.

There are some who have worked for me – in PR – who haven't known the sections of a daily news publication, whether print or online. They simply cannot be bothered to find out that information for themselves. That doesn't work well with my doggedness for delivery, desire to exceed expectations, and my absolute passion and zest to handle all issues with everything I have.

Gen Y is not sufficiently collaborative. When instructions are given to staff to work with a client – and there are the occasional glitches – they need to come back to the initiator and try to sort them out. Often this doesn't happen. In law or bookkeeping, there are always precedents for guidance. In PR, the initiator is there as a precedent, and one would expect staff to report to that initiator when there is a problem. Sadly, many in Gen Y are the product of hurried thinking, hurried pace, iPhone in the ear and SMS at their fingertips. All that augurs for a racy kind of freneticism that has become a cultural habit.

In my years as a worker, a staff member and business owner, I have never seen myself as just passing through. I have always considered myself as stoic and solid, with feet firmly planted on the ground no matter the challenges. I was tenacious, and that is missing in many young people. They demonstrate a lack of stamina and staying power.

It irks me when staff members don't try hard enough to add value for a client. And part of the reason is they are not suitably prepared. We are all apprentices in what we do and there is a learning curve we need to follow. For that we must always be prepared. It is so true in PR; if you are on a tram, bus or train, you should be reading a newspaper or topical magazine; while driving you need to listen to the news and talkback. You must be up to date with what's unfolding. And by that I don't mean constantly checking Twitter, Instagram or Tik Tok!

I have had staff who were not even comfortable on the telephone. Yet, they chose PR as a career!

It is important to be instinctive in PR. You're always writing words or trying to sell a message on behalf of a client, so if you don't pull back and think it through and make that message a part of you, it will lack the necessary sharpness in delivery.

Yes, I have a reputation, as some have claimed, for setting the bar high for my staff. But I wanted the best for my clients, and I expected my staff to think and function along those lines. If I find my staff not stepping out of their skin, as it were, to add value for a client's account, it bugs me.

I had a staff member who saw the downside in nearly everything she handled, despite my instructions to her to 'flip it over' and pull out a precious gem. I am a firm believer that there is a little bit of an X-factor in everything we deal with.

That's why, when mentoring young people, especially young women, I look for that X-factor in them. And I work hard to instil values in them that are going to help them be better people and help them to serve others for the rest of their lives.

Perhaps that explains why I have so often enjoyed mentoring young women of migrant backgrounds. I can relate to their journeys. But I find them free of the self-entitled attitude that I find in too many of their peers. Maybe their parents have impressed on them the value of a strong, honest work ethic.

***

I was so happy when I gained the People Portfolio at City of Melbourne because one of my best attributes has always been my ability to relate well with people. Whether they're eight or 80, I have always been able to talk, share a meal, or even give people a fillip when they're down.

Looking back, at a time when PR companies were all run by men wearing safari suits, I did brilliantly from day one. If women are prepared to put themselves out there, if their intent is clear and honest, if they do all the homework and get around and spread their story, they can succeed.

Don't get me wrong, sexism exists in some shape or form, but at one point in time there were only men to select from – and that's why the boards are as they are. Boards won't change because of gender equity rules; those rules have lifted people's, especially leaders', consciousness, but I don't think we need to be so loud about the rules. These changes will happen as more women become high achievers in business and in study.

During my last term as a Councillor, there were five women on Melbourne City Council, but let's take a look at Parliament: if women don't put up their hands, we can't just say that's because there is bullying. We've got to try to push through bullying. Yes, it does intimidate us; I've experienced it. But politics is still a career path women can follow, one for which they need female and male mentors to guide them along the way.

There are too many traps for women, especially young women, along the way. And we need to be focusing much more as a society on how we support our teenage girls – no matter what career path they want to follow.

***

Several years ago, I was deeply saddened to read of two girls from Melbourne's eastern suburbs hanging themselves after entering into a chilling suicide pact. The girls, close friends, were both 16. They had seemingly happy lives, doing what most girls that age do – experimenting with makeup and quirky fashions. They had an eye for boys, liked the latest rock music and, tellingly, delved into the dark side of the internet where they found sites devoted to assisting people to kill themselves.

In an interview on Channel Nine's *60 Minutes*, the father of one of the girls said, "I am Dad, I can fix anything . . . I have always been able to fix whatever has gone wrong." That's the fatal mistake parents can make; they wait until something has gone wrong to fix it.

Sixteen is a very difficult age for most teenagers. I remember it well, especially my strict upbringing and the pressure from my eldest brother, Errol, who took his chance to bully me whenever my parents were not around, making my life a living hell.

Because my parents were busy working long hours to make ends meet, I felt neglected. I had also changed schools after my parents bought in Springvale and, as I explained earlier, I encountered racism at Springvale High School. Fortunately for me I had a distraction – vying for recognition and acceptance in the new country I called home. I needed to perpetuate my dream of becoming a princess. That's when I became involved in the quest of being crowned a beauty queen and fundraising for charities associated with some of the contests. I found something bigger than myself to be involved in. And, of course, I was mentored along the way.

I was very fortunate to become involved in Aboriginal activist Harold Blair's efforts on behalf of Aboriginal children. His attitude motivated me to go out and help raise money for his project, ensuring I had a life outside home and school. The fact that many parents don't involve themselves in their children's lives is sad. It's when children can go astray and, when their parents step in, it is often too late, as was the case with the two young girls I mentioned.

After hearing of their deaths, I developed a diagram called a Portrait of Influence that accounts for what I call Structural Integrity.

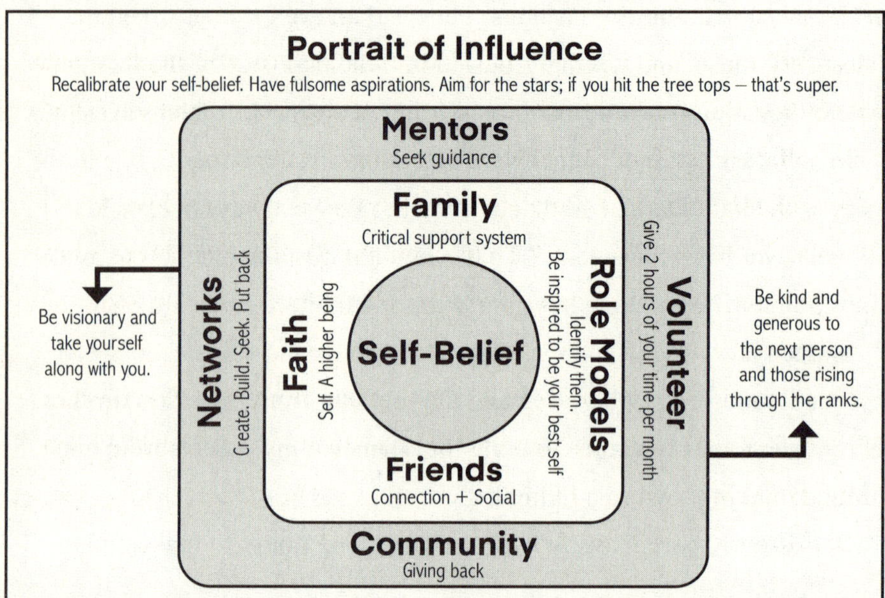

As you can see, at the core are the two teenagers' sense of self-belief. They are surrounded by family, in one of the girl's cases it is a fractured unit because her parents were separated, and her father had remarried. Both girls' parents were loving but hadn't offered them life direction. And perhaps they didn't have friends from part-time jobs or sport, a factor that could have influenced their lives.

Surrounding this in my diagram is volunteering or charity work, which is what I turned to when I was 14. It helps keep one's mind occupied and freer of harmful distractions. Then there is the outer frame that defines the need for other influences, such as mentors.

The girls' cores were unstable. While they had loving families, they didn't have much in the way of direction. When someone says, "I am going to kill myself", you need to heed that cry for help. I had someone there for me when I reached that low point in my life. And that's when mentoring becomes a very vital part of our lives.

My views on this stage of a young person's development are strongly influenced by the Hoffman Process, which helps individuals discover their true essence, by discarding negative attitudes or behaviours that they grew up with.

Created over 50 years ago by Bob Hoffman, the process aims to create more love in the world, in each of our lives, healing the rifts in our beings that result from not being unconditionally loved as children.

Hoffman developed a program which looks at 'negative love patterns' that we instinctively learn from our parents. We either adopt these patterns, or rebel against them, creating more intricate and complex patterns.

We are not used to thinking or processing our thoughts and actions in this way. Recognising these patterns and how they impact on us and how to deal with them is critical to living a calmer, more understanding and loving life on a day-to-day basis.

This process is a combination of psychological practice, mindfulness and spirituality.

Although its impact was not immediate when I engaged with the Hoffman Process some 33 years ago, it resonates strongly with me and two family members who have participated in it.

***

Shortly before this book went to print, I heard a news report that 13 young people – all under 18 – had committed suicide in Victoria in the first quarter of 2023. Nine boys, four girls.

This is more than double the number of suicides for the corresponding period last year. In previous years, there had been between 15 and 23 youth suicides for the whole year. So this is an alarming trend. Moreover, there is a troubling increase in the number of hangings. Hanging has become more prevalent as a means for (young) people to take their own lives.

This must be devastating for the parents of these children. What can parents do to prevent such tragedies?

I believe that connectedness to family and friends is critical.

Sometimes the reasons may be identifiable and applied to particular geographical areas, but at this stage, no particular indicators have been picked up as to where these have occurred or even why.

Prevention opportunities may be identified and access to services is critical.

The last few years have been hard for all of us a consequence of the Covid lockdown years, especially in my home state, Victoria. Coming out of Covid and returning to normal is no less difficult. People are dealing with one or more resulting challenges: mental health issues, marriage pressures, financial pressures including loss of business turnover, and rising interest rates for business loans and mortgages. Not to mention the recent jumps in rents, and lack of available rental properties.

The best message I can suggest is: Stay in touch; Stay connected.

We need to look out for the young people in our lives. Give them support and as much care as we possibly can.

Support and services are available - but the most important safeguard is family and friends. Look out for those who are troubled and concerned. That will give you the best chance to hear from them first-hand if they are contemplating self-harm.

Parents and families need as much information as they can about the risk.

They need to know what the warning signs are: identify the risk, identify the means so they can offer the best support possible.

According to the State Coroner, Judge Cain, this is a conversation that we as a community need to have. Parents and friends need to be armed with information and shared observations.

Resilience is an important life skill. How do we as a community encourage younger generations to value and develop it?

***

In 2008, when she was Minister for Education, Julia Gillard proposed that Australia's top 100 companies should adopt schools to offer advice, mentoring and work experience. The concept gained the support of some of Australia's biggest companies, such as BHP Billiton, Coles-Myer and National Australia Bank. Under the plan, each company would partner with a mix of well-off and battling schools, under the auspices of the Business Council of Australia.

In an interview with Melbourne's *Herald-Sun* newspaper, Ms Gillard said: "Our top 100 companies are full of people with skills, energy and enthusiasm. Let's match them with schools so every secondary school benefits."

Australia has about 2650 secondary schools, so each leading company would have to 'adopt' about 27 schools, offering their expertise to school councils in areas such as accounting and IT. And senior staff would be linked with students in need of role models.

Ms Gillard's concept had great merit. It has scope to provide good mentors for young people looking for direction in their lives.

***

I have been able to be a positive influence in the development of my godson, Ashley. He was having problems at school and was somewhat lacklustre in his academic performances. Since he was five years old, I have been talking to him about how, despite not enjoying academic success myself, I was able to "conquer the world" in my business. Now, aged 38, he works at Microsoft following a successful stint at Amazon, and prior to that the University of South Australia.

I did the same kind of mentoring in 2004 with my then 13-year old former neighbour, Maddie. I met her in the lift of our apartment building. When she became all teary after her parents wanted her to stay fit by running, I started a walking club every Wednesday night instead – and she loved it. She was very creative and wanted to explore stage acting, but success for each of us is different. In our teens we may not know what success looks like, but we need people around us who will nurture our dreams rather than quash them. Otherwise, young girls may not get the opportunity to enjoy careers like I have.

Maddie represented all I was at her age – kind, effervescent, caring and positive; always ready to lift others' spirits. With a determination to conquer the world, she wanted one day to own her parents' business and replicate their success.

Maddie said she didn't need a university degree or diploma to do it.

I too knew university was not for me. But I was determined to succeed despite having failed matriculation (Year 12 VCE equivalent today). Maddie was determined to finish her VCE, as one milestone on her path to success.

Maddie showed me that a young girl's journey in today's fast-moving world is a difficult one. From juggling the pressures of school to trying to be a model daughter for parents, life is filled with so many stresses that sometimes even the more positive kids can crumble.

Maddie's focus wandered one day when she had a knife in her hand and, while slicing a loaf of bread, it slipped and pierced her left hand, near her thumb. "Did I do that on purpose?" she asked herself. "Is this the attention I need?" Convincing her dad she would never let her mind stray again when she had a knife in her hand, Maddie continued her journey, yearning for her mother's sympathy and love.

She believed that being the elder of two girls was difficult, and she wondered what it was like before her sister, Georgie, arrived on the scene. She yearned for quality time with her mum. Over breakfast one morning in a café near where we lived, Maddie told me she would like nothing more than her mother to invite her out to 'brekky'.

Maddie's joyous personality was infectious. Here was a young girl who could make friends at the drop of a hat. At a Christmas party, several occupants of neighbouring apartments attended and there she was Maddie again, this time with her sister, Georgie, keen to put on a performance. "You were the only adult who encouraged us," Maddie remembered. I'd said, "Come on girls, do us a song", and that was all they needed to get going and perform.

When she had to start at a new school, Maddie was convinced her world had crashed, and she was filled with fear about leaving her friends. I had dinner with her one evening and talked to her about when I had changed schools after my family had emigrated to Australia. Maddie listened and became encouraged. And she worked on making new friends even before the school year started: she did her research and found that one of her current school friends had a friend at her new school. So Maddie forged a relationship online with a girl she had never met, confident this was the best way to ease her transition to the new school.

The new friendship blossomed over two months of the summer holidays and it made it so much easier for her when she entered the school gates. By the end of her first school week, she had immersed herself in her new school and already had a swag of new friendships. She was ready to face any challenge – and she soon got one.

One of Maddie's teachers decided she was too funny and distracting at school, so she labelled her the 'class clown'. At a parent-teacher interview, the teacher mentioned it to her parents. "They were soon treating me like my teacher did," she confided to me.

She withdrew and cried a lot. I told Maddie she needed to crunch this situation with her teacher by writing her a letter telling how she felt when she said unkind words to her. Maddie went one better and spoke to her teacher about the lack of respect shown to her. Rather than turning the confrontation into a no-win situation, she was keen to extract a result from her courageous move to talk to the teacher.

"I told her I would prove that I can concentrate and be a good student as well as be funny," she told me.

It worked and, importantly, the teacher also learnt something from her: "Maddie, you have proven me really wrong. I am never again going to call another student the class clown," the teacher told Maddie.

When Maddie told me all this, I was impressed by her ability to garner the right resources to overcome her challenges. And I was proud to have played a small part in these critical times in her life.

When I asked her the three things she would cite as critical for parents in relating with their children, she said:

Take the time to ask your children how they are going with their girlfriends and boyfriends. Do not shy away from asking about boyfriends; young girls want to talk to their mothers about boys.

Try and understand your eldest daughter's needs and support them through their school days of boys, bitchiness at school, the pressures of study and forming new friendships.

Have the occasional girls' night out with your daughters and exchange views and love. What she called 'quality time'.

Maddie eventually became School Captain. I had urged her to visualise this and make it happen for herself. And she did!

Chapter 16

MY AUSTRALIA: MORE PRIDE THAN PREJUDICE

In order to emigrate to Australia, my family had to satisfy the requirements of the anachronistically-named White Australia Policy. This was one of the fundamental policies of the newly-formed Commonwealth Government, back in 1901.

Despite the presence of aboriginal Australians when British colonisation began, the men who governed Australia saw the new nation as an extension of England, the most distant outpost of the British Empire.

And they made no secret of their desire to maintain the racial purity of Australia, by strictly limiting the number of non-European immigrants (people of Asian or African descent, with colored skin) who would be allowed to come in.

With such an introduction, people often assume that I bear the scars of racial discrimination. They are visibly surprised when I tell them that in my experience, Australia is NOT a racist country or society.

One reason for this is that, to make the obvious point, my family WAS allowed to enter Australia. We found a new home here and enjoyed a quality of life we would never have imagined in Sri Lanka.

The White Australia Policy still existed in the '60s, but the government of the day was slowly, quietly taking it apart, allowing families like mine with a 'high percentage of white blood', to enter. Obviously, we were not fully-white but our Western ways and English being our 'mother tongue' helped greatly in this assessment as did our genealogy and the potential for integration. Never mind that the Southern European migrant of the day was not so keen to assimilate nor did they always speak or try to learn English. They were 'factory fodder' and this proved to be their value to Australia – the 'land of milk and honey'.

The government at the time was also involved in the Colombo Plan, which developed economic and social ties between members of the British Commonwealth, notably by encouraging students from other countries (such as Sri Lanka, Singapore and South Africa) to complete their tertiary education in the UK or Australia, with the assistance of scholarship.

So, while the White Australia Policy wasn't changed overnight, the attitudes behind it were being changed gradually. The ethnic base of Australia's immigration intake had broadened gradually through the 1950s and 1960s, a process that has continued through to the present.

To me, the key to the success of Australia's immigration policy has been the change in emphasis from assimilation, to integration.

For a migrant family whose physical appearance was so different, the idea of assimilating – blending in without anyone realising that we were recent arrivals – seemed crazy. But we did manage to integrate successfully, albeit with an accent that was somewhat alien to the average Aussie.

We didn't change our appearance, or forget the cuisine or customs we had been brought up on. But we did our best to fit in - at school, at work, with our neighbours, in our local community – to show that we were good people who wanted to be good citizens and wanted to learn and understand the customs of our new home. To me, that is what integration means.

I dearly wanted to belong. I longed to learn and absorb as much as I could, so that eventually I could give something back to this nation that was giving my family the priceless chance to enjoy a more comfortable life.

Beverley, Bob Hawke and Yianni Kouros at the Greek Festival in Melbourne's Lonsdale St with good friend Mina.

Day one – start of Beverley's business on 5 June 1985 and 'opportunity came knocking' on the door.

Beverley stands proud following a negotiation to take on the Rowland business in 1993.

by Vilma Wimaladasa

Towards a bright future for 900 Tsunami hit children in Dickwella

Sri Lankan born Beverly Pinder beauty queen, P.R. Consultant, and caring worker for HELP Sri Lanka (Inc), arrives here from Melbourne today (17) to get it all going with a bang.

Her hectic working life, managing a successful public relations consultancy in Melbourne, Australia, hasn't stopped Beverley Pinder from doing her bit for Sri Lanka, the motherland she left 39 years ago.

The managing director of Rowland Pinder, she will be in Sri Lanka today with Susan Riley, the former deputy Lord Mayor of the Melbourne City Council and patron for HELP Sri Lanka Inc, for the opening of a new school wing for the Dickwella North Maha Vidyalaya on Monday, March 19. Also joining her is Joe Schokman, president of the Melbourne-based Sri Lanka Association of Victoria.

As the committee member responsible for fundraising for HELP Sri Lanka Inc.,Beverley is passionate about charitable endeavours, particularly involving Sri Lanka. So when the devastating tsunami struck Sri Lanka she was in the forefront, using her tremendous business and social networks to highlight the plight of thousands of Sri Lankans affected by the killer waves.

Eight schools in the Dickwella area were destroyed by the tsunami, with the Dickwella Maha Vidyalaya suffering the backlash of increased student numbers. Beverley was able to bring together the City of Melbourne, the Sri Lanka Association of Victoria and her own HELP Sri Lanka Inc to raise much-needed funds for the construction of two new levels to the school. It would open the door for 700 children an education that was interrupted by the tsunami. The total project cost is in excess of A$150,000.

The construction was project managed by Architects Without Frontiers Australia.

But there's more! Beverley has secured a A$9000 contribution from Gladstone Park Secondary College, Craigieburn South and Greenvale Primary schools for a science lab. She , has also successfully negotiated with King's College in the UK to support a nutrition programme with the building of a kitchen within the school grounds.

Another A$5000 from Gladstone Park Secondary, the sale of a cricket ball fe ing Murali's signature alon with three other leading wi takers, will enable the new kitchen to be equipped wit utensils and foodstuffs.

No wonder then the forn Miss Australia (she repres Australia at the Miss Unive Pageant in 1978) added to t many accolades she has received over the years wh she was awarded the title o Female Sri Lankan of the at a glittering ceremony la year organised by Serendib News, a Melbourne-based S Lankan newspaper publish by Virosh Perera.

The award was presente the Victorian State government's former Minister for Multicultural Affairs, John Pandazapoulos.

While in Sri Lanka, Bev will also participate in a fu day public relations works with Rowland Bates's MD, Nimal Gunewardena.

Beverley along with her pals Susan Riley, Joe Foenander, the Late Keith de Kretser and Nihal de Run helping in the aftermath of the tsunami in 2005.

'Crowned Miss Australia' Beverley Pinder, Archibald Portrait 2014, painting by Rachel Rovay; photography by Tameika Brumby.

Beverley, Marina de Niese and Sharron Paulse friends since the '60s.

Beverley and Sally Grero, childhood friends and best buddies.

Beverley, Marie Lakos and artist Rache Rovay – friends from Elwood High.

Melbourne's wheelers and dealers: Paul Guerra (VCCI), Natalie O'Brien (MCEC), Beverley, David Mann (3AW), Josephine Foo and Susan Riley.

Beverley with one of her best buddies, Arron Wood AM, former Deputy Lord Mayor, City of Melbourne (2018-2020).

Father Bob and Beverley at one of the many fundraising initiatives she helped organise for the Father Bob Maguire Foundation, aboard the Lady Cutler in December 2021, graciously sponsored by Jeff Gordon, owner of the Lady Cutler.

Affectionately known as DB, David Bardas is synonymous with the creation of the Sportsgirl brand and philanthropy. David has been a great mentor, friend and champion of Beverley's for well on four decades.

Beverley and Jack Cyngler – a friendship o more than five decades.

Beverley's godson, Ashley, whom she is proud to have mentored over 35 years.

Kat Izzard and Beverley first connected to promote Melbourne Day and to advance one of Beverley's brilliant ideas, the Junior Lord Mayor competition.

Father Bob with His Excellency Most Rev Peter Comensoli; Archbishop of Melbourne, at the Premier's Iftar dinner, 2022.

Beverley and husband Russell Mortimer, on a glorious autumn day at Government House, when Beverley received her OAM at the 6 April 2023 Investiture.

Beverley's mum, Olga, whose tenacity, hard work and sheer determination to beat the White Australia Policy paid off for the whole family.

I often think there was a synergy, something more than mere coincidence, in the fact that it was Joy Snedden who encouraged me to enter my first beauty contest. (See Chapter 3). Because it was her husband, Billy Snedden, who approved our application to emigrate to Australia, and signed the papers that made my parents (and therefore, all of us) Australian citizens.

Sir Billy Mackie Snedden, as he later became, was leader of the federal Liberal Party, and Leader of the Opposition, from 1972-75, and served as Speaker of the House of Representatives from 1976-83. Earlier in his career, he held several Cabinet positions, including Minister for Immigration, from 1966-69. It was this last role that made his name, and his signature on official documents, familiar and important to me.

Ironically, in later years, we moved in similar circles, and had a number of mutual friends, but never met. Even so, I still associate Sir Billy and Lady Joy with the opportunity and encouragement that Australia offered me.

A point on racism: I get a little annoyed when earnest, well-meaning commentators, politicians and anti-racism organisations stir up trouble unnecessarily.

For example, if somebody makes a comment about Sri Lankans, let me and any other Sri Lankan decide for ourselves whether or not those comments were racist or offensive. It is when the discussion is led by those lacking in colour or difference that it goes awry and makes out as if we today have a major problem with racism.

Our resilience and our ability to also share a joke is underestimated when we have others speaking on our behalf. It's possible that we might just agree with whatever was said, then get on with our lives! This coming from a girl who was referred to as 'Cinnamon' for a good one-sixth of her life. Cinnamon, caramel, latte or brown, may Nazeem Hussain and Dilruk Jayasinghe (who both hail from Sri Lanka) reign supreme with their brown jokes, and may they change the way the world celebrates us.

***

The way I feel about Australia – my adopted homeland, the country that welcomed me and my family – is summarised in a speech that I was honoured to give as a City of Melbourne Councillor, at a Citizenship Ceremony in Melbourne on Australia Day, January 26, 2014.

"Australia is big, with wide, open spaces. It is welcoming, and it has the most relaxed, most beautiful people. As a nation, it is generous to us all. It gives us privileges, with lots of room to expand and grow, and opportunities aplenty.

"Go after your dreams, and you can achieve them here. Never stop dreaming. Because Australia gives you back tenfold for the effort you put into your daily lives.

"All the while, know that a big part of being Australian is also being generous to your community. As you grow healthier, wiser, richer, and become more and more Australian, take time to stop, and give back to those who are vulnerable: the sick, the elderly, the disabled, those experiencing homelessness. They need your thoughts and actions. So I welcome you, but I also urge you to take on the challenge of being the very best Australian you can be."

I feel fortunate, blessed, that Australia welcomed me and my family when I was a young girl. Australia gave us a new home, and opportunities that gave us a chance to prosper. I have always felt grateful for that opportunity. And because of that feeling of gratitude, I have always felt an obligation to pay it forward. Not just an obligation, it has always been a pleasure to extend some help to those who need it, when I have been in a position to help.

To me, that is what being a good Australian is all about. Today,

Australia is a flourishing, multicultural nation, and my pride in her and her people knows no bounds. Australia has given me more opportunities than I would ever have received anywhere in the world: I am so very proud of her!

Chapter 17

MENTORING YOUNG WOMEN

Reflections from some of the young women I've mentored, and other valued friends

Mentoring young women has been one of the most inspiring and important things I have done in my life. I'm so happy to be able to share with you just some of my mentees' reflections on what it was like to have me as their mentor. I have also included words from several long-time friends, reflecting on our friendship.

Mina Italiano: A Great Relationship After So Many Years

"I've known Beverley since I was 18. I met her when I was a receptionist and centre secretary at Southland Shopping Centre. Westfield had just bought Southland and Beverley was Westfield's PR consultant, so I met her that way.

"I liked Beverley from the get-go. She was dynamic and full of energy, she got things done. She delivered on her promises, and I loved the way she connected with her clients. When Beverley says she's going to do something, she does it. I really liked her style of working and we just hit it off.

"When I was 21, I went and worked with her as her personal assistant and office manager. That was when her business had just started and she was in Queens Road, Melbourne. She had other staff, but no one to run the office. I worked for her initially for five years when her business was in its infancy, then took skills I'd learnt with her into working with our family business, especially regarding launching products. Then I went back to work with Beverley again and it was exciting to see how her business had grown.

"The thing I learnt most from Beverley was attention to detail. A lot of the press releases and other work was very manual in those days and could be laborious. But her attention to detail was always spot on – and that is something that has served me well in any job I've had in my career. Building a relationship with Beverley and working with her meant I learnt skills that I couldn't have learnt anywhere else at that time.

"She was ahead of her time in lots of ways, being a woman and going out on her own in a PR business. I saw that she'd work for clients as hard as she could until she got the job done, always focused on delivering for them, never focused on herself. And she was also ahead of her time in the way she built relationships with media.

"She had a way of making clients feel they were her *only* client – even though we had a long list. We were always incredibly busy with so much to do, but I never felt we were failing to deliver for any of our clients.

"I absolutely love the fact that Beverley and I still have a great relationship after more than 35 years. When we worked together, it was like I was her little sister, but now we guide and counsel each other. I will always ring Beverley if I'm uncertain about something and need a sounding board, and she knows she can do the same with me. She's always been a mentor, a confidant and a friend and someone I can bounce ideas off.

"Whether I have been working with her or not, I've always had a sense of belonging with Beverley. She taught me respect for people who run small businesses and the learnings they have gained through doing that.

"We worked hard together and, away from work, Beverley is generous to a fault. Whether that was the Christmas parties we had or the outings she took staff on. She has also been generous, not just through business, but through the pro bono work she has done with her charities and her work as a Councillor. She just gives beyond what anyone could ever expect of her."

Mina Italiano is EA Advocate, Co-founder/Partner, Sorelle Event & Network Consultants, and CoChair, trib.Australia

Madelaine Geraghty: An Unstoppable Beauty

"Beverley Pinder is an absolute queen. She is my friend; she is family and she is my mentor.

"I was about 12 when I met her. My family had just moved into the Scala apartment building where Beverley lived. I was immediately drawn to Beverley's friendliness and confidence – and her dog, Jackson, this cute little white dog that looked like a cloud!

"I visited her apartment and there was a huge framed photo of her being crowned Miss Universe, Australia, and I just immediately thought, *Wow!*

"She treated me and talked to me as an adult, not a child. I saw Beverley as my first real, grown-up friend.

"As I grew into a teenager, I struggled a lot to communicate and get along with mum. Beverley helped me a lot through this time and knew exactly what to say to cheer me up. This was a difficult time for me, being a hormonal, annoying, dramatic teenager – I was complaining and crying to Beverley, a woman who at the time did not have children of her own. She somehow always had the time to listen. I admire how, even though I was upset and talked about mum and all the other drama that teenage girls go through, Beverley never disrespected my mum.

"Beverley taught me to have confidence and to not care what others think. She also taught me to love the skin I am in and the person that I am. Beverley taught me about patience, and this really helped when she offered advice about my relationship with mum. She would always assure me that I just had to be patient and once I matured and experienced life a little bit more, my relationship with mum would get better and stronger.

"I know I have taken on professional and personal traits that Beverley inspired in me. I did my high school work experience with Beverley's PR company, so I was able to see the work side of Beverley's life. I learnt from her to be a 'go getter', never take no as an answer and to, most importantly, choose a career that you love because if you hate your job then you are going to have a very miserable Monday to Friday lifestyle.

"And she taught me about beauty routines! Beverley was always onto me about my skin when I was younger. She would give me her beauty tips on how to properly wash my face and clean my skin! It might seem like nothing, but it did mean a lot at the time for someone to notice that my skin was a cause of insecurity, and to help me and show me how I could improve my appearance. It was huge for a teenage girl! Beverley has the best, cleanest skin in the universe, so her skin and beauty tips really do work!

"Beverley has confidence and beauty, but she is also just a genuinely lovely person, which to me is such an important trait to have. I don't know how she does it, but this woman can literally do anything she puts her mind to! It amazes me how she has this drive at life to keep going and to not stop, no matter what gets in her way.

"She does not live in the same building as me anymore. However, we have the type of friendship where we don't have to see each other every day, but when we do see each other, we just pick up from where we left off. I love our friendship and she will always have a special place in my heart!"

Madelaine Geraghty, Behaviour Support Practitioner, Centre for Positive Behaviour Support

Andalis Yin: An Ideal Image to Follow

"As an international student, working with Beverley was the most meaningful and enjoyable time for me in Melbourne.

"I undertook a three-month internship at Rowland Pinder, where I became accustomed to the Australian workplace for the first time. With Beverley's help, I gained numerous professional skills, as well as some good habits that impacted me a lot, such as setting up a work-in-progress chart to increase efficiency.

"Due to the uncertainty of my health condition, I have to travel back to China for follow-up check-ups every six months. I remember the day I told Beverley about my situation; she spent almost an hour searching for the information and the treatment of my condition.

"Beverley has been a mentor not only in my internship, but also for my life. During the three-month internship, Beverley taught me, educated me, guided me and, most importantly, inspired me. Besides helping me polish my professional skills and become a qualified employee, Beverley cultivated me as a confident, strong and independent woman.

"I found that Beverley was always playing the role of a mentor in people's lives. During my internship, we had a client who was also a young Chinese girl trying to establish her own business in Melbourne. Because she was unfamiliar with Australian business models, Beverley established a mentorship as part of Rowland Pinder's partnership with her. And, even after we ceased our contract, Beverley still thought of her whenever an opportunity came up that could be helpful to the girl and her business.

"For me, Beverley presents the ideal image of the kind of person I want to become."

Andalis Yin, having returned to China for ongoing medical treatment, is now Media Master at Wavemaker China

Eunice Wong: Tough Love and Respect

"Beverley Pinder is the toughest yet most genuine person I know. She gave me the opportunity to venture into Public Relations. She believed in me and trained me up to not only be the best, but also the most reliable support and PR person for my clients and colleagues.

"Beverley is the epitome of tough love. She stretched me to my utmost potential and taught me to seek my deepest core for solutions and to think laterally. She made me realise what my weaknesses were so that I could hone and perfect my skills.

"She helped me fully understand the importance of design, web management, profile building, marketing, project management and finance management, helping me learn of industries I never thought I would have the chance to absorb.

"Her criticisms were strong, and there were definitely times I doubted myself, yet I know her criticisms are what built me up in skills and personality. She pushed me to strive for the best opportunities that I could find for clients, stakeholders, partners and suppliers. I took all of these learnings in, knowing they would be beneficial for my skills and expertise in future, which has proven to be true for my career thus far. I also came to understand political campaigning and project-planning because I was with her when she first ran to be a Councillor at City of Melbourne.

"It was tough being under her wing; expectations were high and there were times I knew I disappointed her. We cried, laughed, joked and yelled at each other. We debated with one another and enjoyed after-work wine together. I would not give up my experience with her for anything, because she poured her time and patience into me to help me grow, both professionally and personally.

"I am grateful for the energy she spent on me. I looked up to her and am thankful she took me under her wing during my time working in

Melbourne, especially when she cooked her lovely Sri Lankan *brinjal* curry for me – gosh how I miss it!

"Beverley instilled empowerment in me – as women, we need to rise above and beyond in the sea of men and rely on our own capabilities to achieve our goals and dreams. She taught me never to be afraid to speak out or stand out.

"I sometimes find myself emulating certain traits of hers while running my business with my partner back here in Malaysia.

"My time with Rowland Pinder was definitely worthwhile, and I still refer to the advice she imparted to me. I could not have asked for a better first work experience than the one I had with Beverley. She was a tough mentor, but she is the most respected and esteemed figure I hold in my heart."

Eunice Wong is Senior Partner and PR Director Southeast Asia at SLPR Worldwide Group in Kuala Lumpur, Malaysia.

Garima Mangal: An Inspiration to Me

"I started working for Beverley within months of moving to Melbourne, and we soon developed a good relationship, one beyond that of an employer and employee.

"I had no work experience, let alone in marketing and PR. I wasn't confident and was often too scared to take leaps. Beverley was quick to see that and gave me a chance to become confident and gain some experience in the Australian workforce. She nurtured me in every possible way.

"Beverley would guide me on what were the right things to say and how to say the things I wanted to in the right way – with absolute attention to details such as hand gestures (with Beverley's style!).

"Communication has been the most important learning while working with her. I would sometimes attend her speeches and record them, look at them several times and, during university presentations and in other places, try to replicate her grace and confidence.

"In 2019, I left Melbourne for a month-long research trip with my university to Myanmar. A lot happened while I was in Myanmar and I began losing my mental strength. This affected my studies and my performance at work. During the whole of 2019, Beverley stepped in as the support I needed from an elder. I had issues finishing my thesis and my visa situation, as an international student, was very complicated, but throughout 2019 Beverley kept telling me that I would come through as a winner.

"When Beverley attended my graduation ceremony and congratulated me, I was extremely emotional. People were surprised to know that my boss was attending my graduation, but there was absolutely no way this celebration could have been complete without my biggest cheerleader. It was as if Beverley graduated with me that day. She had invested so much of herself in my journey as a young professional. My emotional bond with Beverley goes way beyond what one would normally have with their boss. She created a space that was so comfortable and secure that I could talk to her about anything and everything.

"Her compassion for humanity is one of the factors that makes her a great public servant. While I was studying international development, I would often be reading about all the wrongs taking place in the world. But seeing Beverley working so hard for the homeless and disabled people in Melbourne would restore my faith that there were some good forces working to fight the world's injustices.

"This is why Beverley is a true inspiration to the people around her.

"I've seen Beverley go out of her way to be there for people and connect the right people for their mutual benefit, with absolutely nothing in it for her. I've learnt the importance of doing – and continuing to do – the right thing, even if it is not rewarding you personally. I've also learnt the importance of hard work from the way she continues to find opportunities and pursue them.

"She has left such an impact on my life that, whenever I'm in an uneasy situation, I pause and ask myself what would Beverley say or do?. The grace with which she carries herself and how she continues to stand tall against all odds make her a tough act to follow, but inspire me to be more like her as I move forward with life."

Garima Mangal is from New Delhi, India. She graduated from RMIT University with a Masters of International Development, completed while working as a Marketing and Administration assistant at Rowland Pinder Pty Ltd. Garima is now a Social Media and Content Specialist for Sentius.

Susan Riley: Mentors to each other

"In my final term as a Councillor and Beverley's second term, we shared the same office for three years. I soon realised we were totally different people. I had the knowledge of Council processes and she definitely had the personality to do what she needed to do in the People Portfolio. Beverley has an infectious enthusiasm beyond anyone I've met. She was always impeccable in her grooming and always eager to assist other women – a real 'people person'.

"Our relationship hasn't always been harmonious. We disagreed on many things, but we would always come to a reasonable understanding about the way forward.

"Sometimes when Beverley spoke her mind to other people, I didn't know whether she really considered their feelings. She had the tendency to be reactive rather than listen. Then there would come a 'calming down' period. I'd work to help her understand where the other person was coming from – sometimes, at least.

"Beverley's also one of the most generous, warm-hearted people I've come across. She has this amazing ability to bring the best out in people, especially young people. She has a way of nurturing and encouraging them. Often that means taking them on as interns and, in the case of foreign students, helping them understand the Australian way of life. That all comes from her background.

"I was very fortunate, through Beverley's generosity, to go to Sri Lanka after the devastation of the 2005 Boxing Day tsunami. That's when I saw Beverley at her most humble.

"She came from really, really poor beginnings. She took me to her neighbourhood where she grew up with her parents, and I would be only one of two or three people Beverley has shown where she grew up. The rundown home where they all lived gave me an understanding of how hard it would have been for a family of seven, not to mention then coming across the world to start again in Australia.

"I always admire how far Beverley has come to be where she is today; a strong, independent woman. She has never lost her human side and, if she could, she'd give away every dollar she had to help someone worse off. Which I experienced in Sri Lanka.

"I consider Beverley to be the 'Google Queen'. Anytime during our Council years that I was going out to meet someone I didn't know, Beverley would ask why I didn't know anything about them. I'd say it's only an appointment and she'd say, "Well, that's not good enough". She'd google away and say, "Look, he's got a bit of a shady past . . ."

"I take everyone at face value until I'm proven wrong, whereas Beverley mentored me in many respects, helping me realise that people are always asking something of you in those situations. That mentoring from Beverley was so important. Even though I thought I was pretty good at understanding people, I'd come unstuck. On a couple of occasions, if Beverley hadn't warned me, I would have probably given away the Town Hall!

"Me mentoring her was more about calming her and helping her recognise that she was only seeing an approach to doing something from one side.

"We still mentor each other. Only a couple of days ago she rang and said, "I've got an appointment with so-and-so, what do you think?" And we talked for half an hour on why she thought this appointment was necessary. That's a really good thing to have in a friendship.

"A lot of people would say to me, 'She is really cutting and abrupt' or 'She needs to learn to treat people as her equal'. But I never saw that in her. The real Beverley is the one doing pro bono work and being generous by helping young students or people experiencing homelessness.

"She sets demanding standards for herself, but Beverley is at her best when she's relaxed. She used to bring a lot of stress on herself. She'd leave a Council committee meeting and go home and stew about it. Then she would come in the next day and blow up. But that stress came from her thinking that we'd done the wrong thing as councillors. Many times she'd say, "I can't vote for this". I'd ask why and we'd work through it, and I'd say, "You don't have to vote for it. If you don't believe in it, don't do it". And she would be the odd one out. Still, she believed in what she believed, so she had to stand up for it.

"It's taken a long time for Beverley to learn to delegate. She went overseas on holidays once and asked me to act as caretaker in her business. That was when I realised our management styles were so different. The staff were scared of her, and they couldn't make decisions on their own. I believed in independency, but Beverley believed in control. With her staff, we'd be in the middle of promoting some big business idea and her staff would be saying, 'We've got to ring Beverley in Italy and find out if it's the right thing to do!' I felt like shaking them.

"By the time Beverley got home in six weeks, the office was different. Beverley said that I had absolutely changed the culture of her office. And she wanted to control them again! Still, everyone I've met who has trained under Beverley has emerged as a true professional.

"Beverley doesn't suffer fools. And I found that out in her approach to staffing and in so much of her decision making. She'd come in and say, "Nup. Not going to work for me." It's often black or white with Beverley.

"I haven't always agreed with Beverley, but we have a mutual respect that we've each earned. We had our differences, but we were able to manage them and come back. And it was that ability to come back from fallings-out that helped our friendship grow.

"I think Beverley over the years has been impatient and frustrated mainly when she has seen bureaucracy blocking her desire to look after people. She is always trying to serve others, not herself. That's why if she ever chose to become a CEO of a charity she would be superb at it. Her passion is giving back to people who need it. She'd never be taken for a ride either – except by ex-husbands!"

Susan Riley served several terms as a Councillor with the City of Melbourne, including terms as Deputy Lord Mayor 2001-04, 2008-16 and as a Councillor 2017-2020.

Rachel Rovay: A lasting friendship

Artist Rachel Rovay has been a good friend and confidant of mine since our days at Elwood High in the late 1960s. We lost touch for 30 years after my parents moved the family to Springvale, but then we reconnected, and continued our friendship.

After finishing at Elwood High, Rachel pursued her passion for Fine Art at Caulfield Institute of Technology (now Monash University), and has gone on to be a highly successful artist.

In 2004, Rachel asked if she could paint my portrait for the Archibald Prize. She said she had always been entranced by my face and what she called my "Mona Lisa smile". The portrait was displayed in August that year at a prestigious art exhibition entitled "The Hidden Faces of the Archibald Prize" at Crown Towers.

Below are some thoughts Rachel wrote about me and painting my portrait:

"By the time I met Beverley again after more than 30 years, I had become an exhibiting artist with my work represented in private and public collections. As always, her face fascinated me with its quiet defiance that dared anyone to unravel it. Her face reminded me so much of Leonardo Da Vinci's enigmatic Mona Lisa, whose portrait has captured the hearts of millions of art lovers over the years. Could Beverley be my *Mona Lisa*? After all, she had her enigmatic smile.

"When she gave me permission to do her portrait for the prestigious Archibald Prize in 2004, I decided to let that mystery unfold, ever so gently. Beverley had done things and achieved much against all odds. To me, it was the ultimate inspiration that made me wonder how unique she was. How many people would have gone under in like situations? Not Beverley, she survived all that. And those were the elements that encompass my portrait of her. They motivated me in terms of colour, structure and rhythm.

"Her achievement in being crowned Miss Australia, a dark-skinned girl pitted against tall, blue-eyed and white-skinned blondes was fascinating, and when I started to work on a series of preliminary sketches I was doing it against the ominous background of a racist undercurrent stirred by the emergence of Pauline Hanson and her divisive brand of politics.

"The portrait is symbolic of the many barriers Beverley had to surmount in life, which is an inspiration to us all. The vertical compositional line was placed to create a sense of space between the subject and the viewer. Thus the question: is she looking at us or are we looking at her?

"I was influenced by the Sfumato technique which Leonardo Da

Vinci employed to blur the line which outlined the forms to merge with one another. Da Vinci used this technique mainly in two features of the face – the corner of the mouth and the corner of the eyes. This technique became rather symbolic for me, where the Da Vinci had Mona Lisa's left eye and mouth deliberately indistinct, letting them merge into a soft shadow. Mona Lisa's expression always seems to elude us, but to express Beverley's inner strength and dignified confidence, her left eye and the corner of her mouth were instead accentuated. Mona Lisa does not have eyebrows, while Beverley's face has defined eyebrows, giving the feeling of strength and achievement. The idea for the column on the right was to use her name and address in Sri Lanka, in the Sinhalese script, which I find fascinating for its beautiful formation within a circle."

Rachel Rovay is an award-winning artist whose works have been included in many public and private collections. She regularly displays new works by herself and other artists at her Gallery in Middle Park, Melbourne.

Sally Grero – My Peer and a Role Model

"Remembering Beverley de Zylva at St Lawrence's School is a fresh memory as yesterday. Our friendship has spanned more than 60 years.

"Beverley was a 'brain box' with short hair and tan in colour. I lost contact with Bev when she left school to migrate to Australia with her family, in the late 1960s.

"Through a happy coincidence, a mutual friend met her at Albert Park Lake while she was jogging and passed on her phone number. We all got together and spent a very happy day, talking and laughing. It was nearly 36 years since we had last met.

"Beverley is a very loyal friend and is always a shoulder to cry on. We respect each other immensely. She is a special friend, one who is filled with kindness and generosity. She is accepting of you no matter where you have come from.

"Bev hasn't forgotten her roots, despite becoming Australia's Beauty Queen in 1978.

"In primary school, Bev was involved in sports and played an active role in school competitions. She enjoyed playing netball and she was great in scoring goals. She used to come early to school to practise and stay after school to gain more confidence on the court.

"Beverley got along with all her school mates ; no matter what caste or religion, she treated all of us the same.

"During our time at St Lawrence's, all students had to participate in the cultivation of paddy - it was compulsory. Called SHAMADANA we had to weed and plough the land – Beverley was among many of us who simply did it and helped all of us feel like we were on the same team.

"Bev is one of the most vivacious people I know.

"She was clever in Maths and English and she was very fluent in her 2nd language, Sinhalese, although she cannot recall any of it now. In Maths, she was the first to solve the problem and always whispered to others how to work out the sums.

"I remember how she read the book *Madol Doova* by Martin Wickramasinghe - she was so eloquent when she read to us. We aspired to read as well as she did.

"The book is a children's novel and coming of age story, first published in 1947. The book recounts the misadventures of Upali Giniwella and his friends on the Southern coast of Sri Lanka during the 1890s. She was very popular with the teachers.

" I am so proud of all of her achievements. Beverley has done well and her work at the City of Melbourne as Chair of the Family and Children's Advisory Committee was exemplary. She is a fine example of a caring person for whom family always comes first. Bev has helped me in numerous ways; I will never forget her kindness.

"I wish her every bit of good luck and happiness in all that she does."

Sally Grero is an old schoolmate from Sri Lanka, who moved to Melbourne several years after my family did. I was delighted to re-connect with her and resume our friendship

Chapter 18

EPILOGUE

As I completed writing this book, a new year is dawning with 2023 appearing on the horizon.

I could barely wait for the calendar to turn to January 26, I no longer needed to keep secret the most exciting news of my life: that I had been nominated to receive a Medal of the Order of Australia!!

I was contacted by a member of the staff of the Governor-General, General David Hurley (AC, DSC, FTSE), to advise me of the nomination, and to check whether I would be prepared to accept this award, which was made in recognition of my support for various charitable organisations. Along with 735 other award recipients throughout Australia, including 506 female Medal of the Order of Australia awardees, my news was announced on Australia Day.

As I hope I have made clear here, I believe that giving your support to charity (whether financial, or in time, energy and ideas) is its own reward.

When I look back to when I was awarded the crown of Miss Universe Australia, that meant so much to me as proof that this young immigrant from Ceylon had been accepted by Australia as 'one of us'. But now that I have been awarded membership of the Order of Australia, it is as official as it can be, that I have been accepted as a citizen of this great, generous nation. And I am so proud.

Twenty-twenty-two is the year when I closed down my business and officially retired.

But I have been as busy as ever.

One project on my to-do list was to complete the process of writing this book, and preparing it for publication. I hope to see its publication in 2023, and I hope to put my skills and contacts to good use, to generate interest in the book, and sales.

I have decided to direct part of the proceeds from this book to Turning Hope into Action Inc (THIA) which I have been working on for my former colleague on the Homelessness Advisory Committee, Lisa Peterson.

Lisa and I worked tirelessly during Covid setting up this organisation (which is awaiting registration by the Australian Charities and Not-for-Profits Commission).

The amazing pro bono work undertaken by lawyer Dakshika Perera of Velox Legal is now at the pointy end where we wish that we can achieve this registration.

It seems like being a 'Voice for the Homeless' is not as attractive as raising money to feed, clothe and 'ignore' the homeless, continuing to have them sleep on the streets with no possibility of advancement. We believe that it is THIA's voice that will help recognise homelessness as a transition and not a destination. A voice for those who are largely not understood by many of whom are in positions of power and authority handing out the funding and devising the policies that are in the main, flawed.

This will be my challenge for 2023-24. It is great however, to know that my good friend and former City of Melbourne colleague, Susan Riley is onboard with us and keen to help us as Chair of the organisation. I have also seconded my good buddy of many decades, the Hon. Bruce Atkinson as Patron.

THIA is a real alternative to the many agencies that provide support to the sector.

The only organisation of people with a lived experience of homelessness working for and supporting those who are 'living the experience', we plan to become the peak body for people experiencing homelessness

Lisa cites homelessness as an experience and not a category of disadvantaged person. Together the three of us are hell-bent on effecting change.

The two key pillars to our work are:

- To be a service of training, support and advocacy to those with a lived/living experience of homelessness,
- To work towards a better system for those who have no choice but to use it through education, advocacy and consulting with the community about the homeless experience.

The Melbourne Men's Shed has enquired of my interest in being its Patron. As this Men's Shed was one of my most significant achievements while at Council, and, as my engagement with members continues to this day, I was recently delighted to accept their invitation to become their Patron.

Additional work includes the many Owners Corporation Committees that I sit on and our extensive property portfolio.

I also am keen to help with the rebuild of Sri Lankan tourism supporting the Lankan Fest organisers and singing the praises of this Jewel of the Indian Ocean.

I continue to seek board appointments, albeit with great difficulty. It seems like these days a degree and alignment with the right political party is what you need to gain recognition. Attributes of experience and expertise in governance, marketing, volunteers, retail operations or small business is simply not enough.

I will continue, with my unabated desires to give of my talents and skills to not-for-profits and energetic, young people who wish to traverse a connected and successful path – it is in my DNA and that is where it will stay. Membership of The Order of Australia Association is the start of a new adventure in my communitarianism adventure.

As I approach the last stretch of my sixties, I have lived a rich and fulfilled life; it is time to relax just a tad, and to impart what I can to others while giving a helping hand to those who need it most – the aged, the disabled and the vulnerable.

Chapter 19

VALE, FATHER BOB

Just before this book was ready to go to print, we received the news that Father Bob Maguire, AM RFD, had passed away on 19 April 2023. As a devout Catholic, I have no doubt that he has gone to meet his maker. And I suspect that he will give the Creator some frank advice on a few things that He could have managed better!

Father's passing was not a surprise, as his health had been deteriorating for some time. Even so, it was a jolt, to think that he would no longer be among us, helping those who most needed help, and dispensing sage advice as only he could.

Father Bob loomed large in my life for well on four decades.

I first met him at a Carlton-Collingwood VFL game during my brief stint as a member of the Carlton cheer-squad, 'the Bluebirds'. He was a guest speaker at a pre-game function, and he commanded the audience's attention with his genuine thoughts and larger-than-life personality.

I had already enjoyed a rich and productive friendship with Father Ernie Smith. He was also a doer of much good for the 'unloved' in our society. In the early '80s, my husband, Peter Cox, and I were among the grassroots volunteers who assisted Father Ernie in the creation of the Sacred Heart Mission - the forerunner to today's well-established Mission in Grey Street, St Kilda. Like Father Bob, Father Ernie dedicated his life to the poor, homeless, sick and marginalised. There would have been no Mission today without Ernie Smith.

As I got to know Father Bob better, I appreciated the honesty, fairness and reason of any advice he offered me. And I was determined to do all that I could to assist him in his efforts to help the less fortunate in our community. Others might have looked down on the jobless, the homeless, the alcoholics, drug addicts and sex workers among us. Not Father Bob. To him, we were all children of God, all part of the same community, and all deserving help, each according to his or her needs.

Father Bob's teachings will be with me for a long time. He knew my family. He was there for my mother's last moments, with the Last Rites being pronounced by Father along with my brother Sandy via phone from Darwin.

Father presided at my mother's funeral service at the drop of a hat, when the parish priest at the church near where she had been living wanted to place various restrictions on the funeral service that my family had in mind.

My Jewish, Buddhist, Christian, Muslim and Hindu friends expressed their delight at attending my mother's funeral and were amazed at Father Bob's presence and how he worked in with my brother Sandy's family - all ten children who sang, drummed, played guitars and celebrated life in a manner in which only Father could stage manage.

Wit, wisdom, humour, care, generosity, kindness and service to his community - the one-of-a-kind stoic larrikin priest gave us his all in a way we will never again witness. Here's to his Sainthood and to 'Communitarianism'. Vale my special friend and faith leader.

I wrote a brief post on Facebook

"My dearest Fr Bob - Rest safely in peace in our Father's arms. Thank you for the many lessons you taught me, in particular this one on the occasion of your birthday on 14 September 2020 – which coincided with my campaign for a third term on Council. My love for you will endure as I continue to enact the principles of 'communitarianism' - one of your many mantras. We will miss you and your indefatigable spirit. Now it is time for the crusader of the 'unloved' to RIP."

***

At the State Funeral Service for Father Bob, held in Melbourne's iconic St Patrick's Cathedral, Victorian Premier, Dan Andrews, said, "Father Bob did not find the community - he built one. Father Bob was someone who understood that we are stronger united than split. Those without a voice or without a home were Father Bob's people. Anyone who turned up on his doorstep got what they needed in that moment."

Bishop Mark Coleridge, Archbishop of Brisbane, regarded Father Bob as his mentor. In his Homily, he said, "Ernest Hemingway once wrote that the world breaks everyone and afterward many are strong in the broken places. Bob was one of the many. He was broken by much of his earlier life, but he grew strong in the broken places, which is why he was able to understand and embrace human brokenness and to learn passionately to bring strength to the broken."

Father Bob was always the outsider who wanted to be the insider.

His Excellency continued: "He was a real human being who rose beyond the brand. His religion was one where faith and good works went hand in hand.

"He was universally loved and admired. He believed in the ethos of the second Vatican Council. He pushed the message that we need to live our lives as a community; which means that we as insiders need to be there for the outsiders. Creating a sense of belonging for those who have and those who have not. He swallowed the gospel whole and lived it.

"He often said, 'There is still much to be done and little time in which to do it.'

"Bob was about action, not just words. He rolled up his sleeves and got stuff done ... he had mud on his boots. He didn't judge or condemn. He opened his door to all. He had an unrivalled and uncontrived sense of humour. Now put that profile together, and you have the kind of religion that has a chance in this country. Put the opposite profile together, and you have the kind of religion that has no chance whatsoever."

The tributes for Father reinforced the central importance of 'communitarianism' to him, and to me.

Communitarian ethics focuses on the importance of the community, and emphasises the influence that community has on human beings. The community a person is born in and raised in shapes their own personality and morality, which implicitly obliges each of us to actively engage in the development of our society.

At the crack of dawn each day, I recall Father's teachings to me. Such has been the impact of this amazing people's person.

***

I had planned to donate all royalties from the sales of my book to the Father Bob Maguire Foundation.

Instead, I have decided that from the launch of the book, and the following six months at least, I will donate part of the proceeds to Turning Hope Into Action. I had discussed this new charity with Father Bob, and it had his enthusiastic support, along with mine. He could see it as an extension of his work.

This could be seen as a protest – a relatively small, and hopefully temporary, one – at the way some matters have been managed by the Foundation's administrators.

If they are going to operate a foundation in his name, they should manage it in a manner consistent with the way Father Bob dealt with people – which was open, forthright and honest.

I need to provide some background, in order to explain that remark -

Father Bob invited me to be a patron of his Foundation, following an $8000 donation for scholarships that my husband Russell and I made a decade ago. That was in addition to my services as event manager for a fundraising lunch, which was assisted by the Hospitality students at William Angliss Institute. With the help of Andrea Cafnik, I persuaded Catherine McGregor to be our guest speaker. Yes, the beautiful cricket commentator, Catherine McGregor AM - a prominent Australian transgender writer, commentator and former Australian Defence Force officer.

Some years later (as mentioned previously), with the approval of the acting Lord Mayor, Arron Wood AM, I asked Father to bless Melbourne Town Hall Chambers at my re-instatement as a Councillor, following the 2018 resignation of Robert Doyle.

I was a proud and active Patron of the Foundation. I didn't worry about what the other Patrons contributed, but I made a commitment to lend my professional expertise and my network of connections, as well as donating as much money as I could manage, to support Father Bob's work. This I did in spades.

Often, I would slip a few $50 notes into Father's shirt pocket. 'Do you want something in return?' he would ask, referring to a receipt for a tax deduction. 'Do as you wish Father', would be my response, knowing that they would be distributed to his community of 'unloved' citizens; after all, we are living in the 'cobber-wealth'.

Perhaps it was only Father Bob and his earnest lieutenant Paul Brophy who knew how much I contributed to the Foundation. So did my friends – who gave generously and supported my fundraising efforts.

So I was shocked and I must confess, offended, to learn the day after the State Funeral Service that I was no longer a Patron of the Foundation. I learned this by visiting the Foundation website to check on some background details, and there it was : a new website, with no mention of me, or any of the other Patrons including Mike Brady and David Galbally.

There was no letter, email or phone call to advise me of this change. In view of the level of support I had given the Foundation as Patron, this was an ill-advised move. Moreover, handled in a thoughtless and tactless manner. One that Father would never have found acceptable.

So that is the context for my decision to take a step away from the Father Bob Maguire Foundation. It may not be a permanent move. I hope that those managing the Foundation will do such a good job that they consistently achieve the goals that the Foundation was established to achieve. If that were to happen, I would gladly resume my support.

Meanwhile, I will focus on doing all I can to support Lisa Peterson and Turning Hope Into Action. More effective assistance for those experiencing homelessness in our community is desperately needed.

And it's funny how it often seems in life that when one door closes, another door opens. Just this week, I was approached by Carl Smith, Secretary of the Melbourne Men's Shed. His email said, "In appreciation of your unrelenting support and advocacy of our Men's Shed over the years, I have been assigned the pleasurable task of approaching you to see if you would consider becoming the Patron of the Melbourne Men's Shed." I happily accepted that invitation.

ACKNOWLEDGEMENTS

- Early Role Models: Uncle Bert, Aunty Tazma
- School friends: Rachel Rovay, Marie Lakos, Jack Cyngler, Simone Baumann, Lyne Cockfield, Persefoni Gouletsas, Sally Grero, Marina de Niese and Sharron Paulse
- Early Influencers: Lady Joy Snedden, Derryn Hinch, Geoff Sinclair, Fr Ernie Smith, Beryl Town, Di Lyttleton, Doris van der Hagen, Bob King Crawford, the late Maurice Perera, who motivated me to start writing this book, Lawrence Machado.
- Sponsors – Business: Tony D'Aloisio AO, Gerald Ryan, Solomon Lew, George Pappas AO, Fabian Dattner AO, David Bardas AO, Ian Murray, Mike O'Neill and Fran Kerlin
- Sponsors – Media: Lawrence Money, Yasmin Willan Scanlon, the late Bill Tindale, Don Baker, Geoff Wilkinson, Neil Shoebridge, Mike Dobbie, the late Leigh Stevens, Peter Cox and the late Steve O'Baugh
- Sponsors – Politics: Robert Doyle, Arron Wood AM, Susan Riley, Hon Bruce Atkinson, Irene Goonan
- Sponsors – Faith: Fr Ernie Smith, Fr Bob Maguire and Brant (Sandy) de Zylva (my brother)
- Eliza Saunders for her advice and careful review
- Kat Izzard, for being a buddy to me over the past decade
- Mark Pagotto, Room 2 Design
- Paul Mitchell, Author/Editor
- My mother Olga de Zylva for instilling in me a work ethic, tenacity and self-pride

I invite any reader whom I might be able to advise or assist in some way, to reach out and contact me. I am a great listener, connector and motivator.

beverley@beverleypinder.com

www.beverleypinder.com